M000200006

Dedication

To the memory of our first friend among the Kogi

Santiago Dingula

Author's Preface

In about October of 1981, I was contacted for an interview with the head of a well-known Christian publishing house. She had heard me speak at a women's meeting, and she encouraged me to write of our experiences as a suburban Minnesota family going to live with a primitive Indian tribe in South America. I told her that I was far too busy to undertake such a project. That was the end of the matter, I thought.

Later in Colombia, my husband, who was in the process of writing a book, said to me, "Why don't you go ahead and try it? It isn't everyone who has a publisher asking them to write a book."

Sometime in 1982, I decided to give it a try. After writing several stories of our interesting experiences in the mountains of northern Colombia, I felt the need to introduce myself to the readers and explain how we happened to be there in the first place. This became a lengthy project. In 1983, our oldest son Russell was kidnapped in Colombia by Marxist guerrillas. I kept notes, and together with my husband wrote a book about this ordeal. My personal story went on the back burner, and it was many years before I picked it up again. I realized that the story was becoming too long for one book, so I decided to break it up into several shorter volumes.

Although three preliminary volumes have been published, the present is a stand-alone volume, the story of a suburban family from Minnesota going to live with a primitive Indian tribe. I hope you enjoy it as much as I have enjoyed writing about our experiences.

A Minnnesota **Mom**

In the Land of
the Ancient Mother

VOLUME I
Beginnings

PATRICIA CARLSON STE

A Minnesota **Mom**

In the Land of
the Ancient Mother

VOLUME II
A Vision is Formed

CIA CARLSON STENDAL

A Minnesota **Mom**

In the Land of the
Ancient Mother

VOLUME III
The Making of a Missionary

PATRICIA CARLSON STENDAL

Synopsis

This book is Volume 4 in the series, A Minnesota Mom in the Land of the Ancient Mother. Volume 2 of this series, *A Vision is Formed*, is the story of a very timid little girl who, by God's supernatural dealings in her life, eventually became a pioneer missionary in the mountains of Colombia. Volume 1, *Beginnings*, gives an overview of the missionary work of the Stendal family, some of the spiritual history of the Stendal/Carlson ancestors, and a short biography of two Indians who risked their lives to invite the Stendal family to live with them on the outskirts of this very reclusive and closed tribe.

Volume 3, *The Making of a Missionary*, tells the story of the Stendal family's training in linguistics at the University of North Dakota, and jungle living at Jungle Camp in southern Mexico. Upon their arrival in Colombia in 1964, an unexpected pregnancy and the birth of their fourth child, Gloria, caused a delay in their assignment to a tribal group. However, the maternity nurse, an elderly Scottish missionary, told them about an unreached tribe of small Indians living high in the mountains of northern Colombia. Chad made a trip to investigate and found that the Lord had gone before and prepared a contact person, Santiago Dingula, who invited them to come live on his small farm. Investigation showed that this invitation was indeed a miracle. No one was allowed to live among these Indians. Chad and Pat made plans to go; however, soon they discovered that their baby had been born with a handicap, a severe congenital hip dislocation. The baby was put into a body cast, which made it impossible to accept Santiago's invitation to come live with him.

The present volume picks up the story in June 1965, as they venture out – handicapped baby and all – to go live on Santiago's farm.

Table Of Contents

Volume IV

Entering the Forbidden Land

Volume IV

Entering the Forbidden Land

To preach the gospel in the regions beyond you

2 Cor. 10:16

And I will give thee the hidden treasures and the well-guarded secrets that thou may know that I am the Lord, the God of Israel.

Isaiah 45:3

After this I saw, and, behold, a great multitude, which no man could number, of all nations and kindreds and peoples and tongues stood before the throne and before the Lamb clothed with long white robes and psalms in their hands.

Revelation 7:9

All quotes from the Jubilee Bible.

Chapter 1

Santiago's Place

San Javier
June 1965

At last the big day arrived. We were off to live at Santiago's house. Our last personal items were packed in duffel bags and tied onto mules. Chad led the way down the trail with Gloria strapped to his backpack, pillow splint and all. A little white bonnet protected her downy blond head from the piecing rays of the morning sun. I was placed on the most reliable riding mule, America, the personal mount of missionary, Edith Leng, and noted for being sure-footed and gentle. Six-year-old Sharon rode behind me on a thin foam rubber cushion. Russell, 9, Chaddy, 8, and Alba, 16, frolicked down the trail. Two "muleskinners," Bible institute students, who were experienced with mules, came along to help us and to drive the pack mules.

Gloria wailed piteously as long as she could see me, but Chad got the idea of sending me ahead, and then she settled down. After leaving San Pedro, we slowly climbed through a meadow to the top of a small pass and then ambled around into jungle foliage. The trail wound up and down, in and out, paralleling a ridgeline on our left. On our right-hand side, the land dropped off. We were now some 3,500 feet above sea level, and now and then we caught sight of the Caribbean Sea miles below. Soon a pattern developed—the trail would curve to the left entering a moist, heavy jungle. A short downhill trot would take us to a small stream. The momentum of the downhill trot would carry us over the stream and halfway up the other side, which now curved to the right. Breaking out into the sunshine again, we would follow along a fairly level trail until the whole process was repeated. Alba and the boys were having a wonderful time swinging on the long swaying vines from the high trees around the streams, playing tag, and throwing stones over the edge and hearing them land far below. Soon Sharon dismounted from the mule to join them. Gloria napped, her head nodding with the rhythm of Chad's pace. My legs became cramped from the unaccustomed position on the mule. I was glad for my previous experiences with mules at Jungle Camp. At least I wasn't frightened of America as I had been of the wild mules at Jungle Camp. As though reading my thoughts, Chad called from behind, "Isn't this place just like Jungle Camp gone mad?"

Actually, we were some of the missionaries who really profited from our Jungle Camp training. Many of our fellow campers ended up in offices or fairly civilized assignments. We, however, needed every bit of our training. I was thankful that I would find a house all ready for our occupancy at the end of the trail. We wouldn't have to build a shelter from scratch as we had at Jungle Camp. One of our Jungle Camp instructors had once told us, "We try to make this training harder than anything you will ever encounter in real life on the mission field. Once you can do it here in a supervised environment, you will not be at a loss in the real situation, no matter how tough it gets." The instructor was right. Had I not had the Jungle Camp experience, I would have been overwhelmed by the prospects of what lay ahead. As it was, my only real concern was for the little handicapped baby who was bouncing along on Chad's back. I knew the other children would be just fine. They had gone to Jungle Camp too.

After several hours we came to the small encampment of San Javier. Women's heads poked out from their mud homes to watch us go by. Someone invited us to stop for a drink of warm soda pop; they had made friends with Chad on one of his previous trips through San Javier on his way to Santiago's farm. These were country Colombian people, non-Indians. Many of them had fled the interior of the country during the 10 years of political violence that had just passed. Others were from the coastal areas of the country. Since many of them were black, it didn't seem quite right to call them *blancos* (whites), the traditional word for non-Indians. We soon got used to the local word in common use, *civilizados* (civilized people).

I too dismounted. We were now on the top of the level ridge. The well-worn trail passed like Main Street between rows of humble dwellings. We would soon be able to see our new home, Chad promised me. My legs were cramped and stiff from the unaccustomed mule ride. I led the mule until Chad said it was time to remount for the next stage of the journey. Far below and on the other side of the river, he pointed out our new house. It looked like a yellow haystack beside the gray, smoke-darkened thatched roof of Santiago's house. Tiny white figures surrounded the two houses. All the Kogis in the area had assembled to witness our arrival.

Now we took a sharp turn to the left and started our descent to the river. Most of the trees had been cut down on this slope, and the trail consisted of a zigzag path of switchbacks through the red clay. I was afraid the mule would slip as Chad's had on his first trip and had gone straight down toboggan style, passing up several switchbacks. I had to practically stand in my stirrups due to the steep descent. Sharon clung to me from behind. The boys and Alba went sliding and slipping down the slope, taking the shortcuts between the switchbacks.

Although the sun was still shining, dark clouds were rolling in from the sea. The muleskinners were anxious to finish this trip before the heavy rains. At last we came to the river and thankfully it was not swollen. Sharon and I crossed on the strong mule, America. I don't know how the others crossed. A muleskinner came behind and urged America up the far bank at a steady fast pace. All of a sudden, we were there!

Chapter 2

Carmelo

Colombia
    June 1965

It had been three long years since our little family of five had left our comfortable home in a suburb of Minneapolis to embark upon a journey of preparation that would take us to the University of North Dakota, southern Mexico, and now to the country of Colombia. Here we would also be joined by the sixth member of our family, Gloria, a baby daughter born in Bogotá, the chilly capital of this South American country, high on an Andean plateau. Since our baby was born with an orthopedic problem, a severe congenital hip dislocation, we had been further delayed from achieving our goal, our purpose for undergoing this training and coming to Colombia in the first place. We had come to live among primitive Indians, learn their language and customs, and adapt as much as possible to their lifestyle in order to share with them the good news of God's love and salvation in their own language.

To equip us in this task, we had studied linguistics for two summers at the Summer Institute of Linguistics (SIL) and completed a course in jungle living in southern Mexico at a place run by the Wycliffe Bible Translators appropriately called Jungle Camp. We had been accepted as junior members of the Wycliffe Bible Translators/Summer Institute of Linguistics, a missionary and scientific organization that made contracts with foreign governments to analyze their indigenous languages and translate books of high moral value.   The goal was to give these previously illiterate people a working alphabet and eventually the New Testament in their own language.

After many delays, we boarded a commercial plane, flying from Bogotá to the coastal city of Santa Marta in the north of Colombia right at the foot of the Sierra Nevada de Santa Marta Mountains where the Kogi tribe lived.   God had miraculously given us an opening in the person of a middle-aged Kogi man named Santiago, who had extended us an invitation to live beside him on his farm and had promised to build us a little thatched-roofed house. A Colombian airline had given our family free round-trip tickets to Santa Marta, and a Colombian teenager, Alba, who wanted to go with us, was on the train and would meet us in Santa Marta. We were now on our way!

This was only the second time I had flown on a commercial airline. As the airplane neared the coast, we could see to the right, far in the distance, the jagged peaks of the Sierra Nevada de Santa Marta piercing the cloud cover. Soon the sparkling blue waters of the Caribbean appeared far below. Gentle waves lapped at lovely sandy beaches. Tall palm trees gently swayed in the breeze.

While watching this spectacular scenery, all of a sudden I was hit by a severe pain in my head. The airplane must not have been pressurized, and my sinuses were stopped up by a recent respiratory infection, thus giving me a very painful descent. In spite of my pain I helped Chad to collect all of our baggage, and we took a public vehicle to the mission house of the Evangelical Union of South America (EUSA). This was the mission that was working in the department of Magdalena. There we were given a hospitable welcome by the missionary couple in charge of the work in Santa Marta, Paul and Barbara Maxwell. Paul and Barbara were Canadians from Alberta and were good friends with one of the professors at the Bethany Missionary Training Center where we were well known. She had written to them about us and to us about them, so it was a real joy for us all to meet one another other.

The next day we walked to the beach for a swim in the ocean. It was a long walk, and Barbara loaned me her parasol. She said that no white women ever went out in the midday sun without protection. Just before we left Bogotá, Gloria had received her smallpox vaccination. This vaccination made a huge open sore, and she picked off any Band-Aid I tried to apply to it. The heat in Santa Marta in June was oppressive, and flies were rampant. Soon Gloria broke out in a heat rash, which also became open sores on her face and arms. I was afraid a fly would sit on her smallpox vaccination and then on one of her other sores and revaccinate her all over her face. I don't know if this was a valid concern or not, but it was a very big worry to me.

It would still be two more days until Alba arrived, so we had to wait for her in Santa Marta. We made a shopping list, and Paul directed us to a good place to buy our provisions. We had been doing quite well with communicating in Spanish in the *Llanos* (the eastern plains where our translation base was located) and in Bogotá, but when we tried to communicate with the storekeeper in Santa Marta, we hit a problem. He couldn't understand us, and we couldn't understand him. We knew that the people in Santa Marta spoke a regional dialect of Spanish called *costeño,* but even that did not seem to explain the complete lack of communication we were experiencing. Finally Chad had to go back to the mission house and ask Paul Maxwell to accompany us. It turned out that the storekeeper was a Chinese man who spoke *costeño* Spanish with a strong Chinese accent. We were speaking Bogotá Spanish with an American accent. Months later, we were able to communicate with the storekeeper.

Finally Alba arrived. She was just a shadow of her former self. She hadn't eaten or slept in four days. We were shocked at her appearance. When asked why she didn't eat or sleep, she said that she saw that the food was being cooked by men, so she wouldn't eat it. She had been told that food cooked by men wasn't any good. She was afraid that if she went to sleep, someone would steal her suitcase, probably a valid concern; however, a good meal and a good night's sleep restored her to her usual bouncy self.

The next day Victor Leng, another Canadian missionary, arrived from Carmelo with the mission jeep. He had a few business errands to take care of in Santa Marta and then decided to transport us immediately up the mountain to Carmelo. After a number of kilometers, we left the pavement and started on a little dirt road up the mountainside. The first step was to ford a small river, about as deep as could be forded by a small 4-wheel-drive vehicle. Then the road went straight up. The land fell off on both sides, and the road continued along a ridge. There was very little switchback on this road, and it was just barely possible to drive the vehicle up the steep mountainside. Later on we were told the story of the long struggle that the Carmelo missionaries had endured to get this road constructed. Ross Clemenger and the first missionaries to found Carmelo carried the building materials up the mountains on their backs. I was so busy holding on to Gloria and bracing myself for the bumps, that I scarcely noticed the magnificent scenery on all sides.

At last we arrived at San Pedro de la Sierra, a little country town at the top of a ridge. We drove through town and cut a switchback down on the other side of the ridge to the right. The road took us straight to Carmelo. The mission buildings were built on terraced levels, and the road took us into the middle level. Along the road to our left were several missionary homes, and to the right, a stairway led up to the top level, the missionary guesthouse. Straight ahead at the end of the road, were the church and the Bible institute. Later we found that down on the lowest level was a large home and school for missionaries' children. The slopes below the buildings, all the way to the river, were planted with crops. Coffee was the cash crop, and yuca, plátanos and bananas provided food for the schools. The men students worked on the farm half days. The woman students worked half days baking bread, gardening, washing the clothes of the men students, and helping out in the missionary homes. The American and Canadian children were on summer vacation when we arrived, but the Bible institute was in full session.

After a delicious supper at the Leng home, we were taken up the side of the mountain to the guesthouse. I told Edith Leng that we could take care of our own meals from then on, and she assured me that a little store right below the guesthouse would be open for a few hours in the morning. Chad told me that all the people at Carmelo were early risers. We had to be up and active at an early hour in order to not be considered lazy, but everyone took a siesta after lunch. We all felt much better in the cool mountain air than we had in the muggy heat of Santa Marta. After a good night's sleep, I went to check out the little store. There I found cornflakes, bananas, eggs, potatoes, onions, and tomatoes. We had brought lots of oatmeal and powdered milk, so breakfast was no problem. I was amazed at the panoramic view that stretched before us from the vantage point of the guesthouse. A steep slope led from Carmelo far down to the river, and then ridge after ridge rose up one behind the other on the far side. The highest ridges faded into a purple haze, which was being rapidly burned off by the rising morning sun. I could see why everyone got up early here on the eastern side of a high mountain.

As I contemplated the series of ridges rising into the sky on the other side of the river, I thought of all the little Kogi people nestled in the nooks and folds of the scenic topography. They were the reason that we were here. Life will be better for them now, I thought with relief. *They will now have a chance to know the Lord because we have come.*

After breakfast Chad and Chaddy started down the trail to Santiago's farm. Chad wanted to see how much progress had been made on our house. He had already run into one of Santiago's non-Indian neighbors who said that Santiago was building a school. It was on this trip that Chaddy refused to cross a log that served as a bridge over a swift river right below Santiago's house. Chad prayed for him, and told him that the Lord would help him across. One of the Bible school students took his hand and led him over the bridge. Chad coming behind noticed that when they came to the end of the log, Chaddy fell off the end. "How come you stumbled off the log?" asked Chad.

"I had my eyes closed," replied Chaddy. If the Lord was taking him across, why open his eyes and be scared, he reasoned. Later on, a neighbor boy slipped on this same log and was swept away to his death by the raging river.

We were amazed that about noon, clouds and a chilly breeze swept up the valley from the sea. Rain fell all afternoon, and the diapers we had washed and hung under the eaves of the house did not dry. "Don't worry," said a teacher who was sharing half of the guesthouse. "All the clothes get dry overnight." Sure enough, about 4:30 p.m. the sun came out again and a dry breeze continued all night. In the morning, all the diapers were dry.

Chad and Chaddy returned from their trip, muddy, tired and happy. They had found four Kogi men in addition to Santiago and Alfonso working on our house. Alfonso's father, José María, his grandfather, Jose Sundungama, Wenceslao, and Miguel were applying mud to the walls of the newly framed building. All that was necessary now was to give the mud time to dry. One of the missionaries warned us against moving in before the walls were thoroughly dry. This was considered to be a very unhealthy situation by the country Colombians and was blamed for all kinds of ills, including pneumonia and tuberculosis.

Alba had been grouchy ever since we arrived at Carmelo. I blamed the train trip for her bad mood, but one day she woke up with both sides of her face swelled up. She had come down with mumps. Since all of us except Gloria had already had the disease, I put her to bed and kept her away from Gloria and the Colombians. She had a mild case and was fine in less than a week.

The stove in the guesthouse was a three-burner countertop gas "plate" without an oven. It was perfectly fine for cooking, but I was a great baker. A day never went by in our family without cookies, cakes, sweet rolls, or "a little something sweet." I credit my Swedish heritage for this custom, or perhaps the fact that at my Grandma Winburn's death when I was 14, I took over most of the family baking. Chad really did not enjoy any baked desserts, but for me no meal was complete without a little treat at the end. I was disappointed to find no oven in the guesthouse.

I state the following to show the Lord's tender care over me, even to pamper me in the little habits that I would later have to overcome. On the bottom shelf under the stove, I found a large box of small, delicious chocolate bars, the best that could be purchased in Colombia. Under the wrapper, each candy bar contained a picture of a jungle animal. These were collectables. Instead of our usual cookies or cakes, the children and I each had a candy bar after dinner. The children enjoyed the animal picture as much as the candy and Chad carried one or two candy bars on his trips to Santiago's house to give him energy on the trail. I finally mentioned to one of the missionary ladies how much I appreciated their thoughtfulness in providing the box of candy bars for us. However, the ladies didn't know anything about the candy bars. They must have been left there by Ernie Granger, the last person to have used the guesthouse, I was told. (Later we brought a box of the same candy bars from Bogotá and gave them to Ernie Granger. He confirmed that it was he who had inadvertently left the candy in the Carmelo guesthouse. He was very happy to receive the replacement, especially as they were "right fresh from Bogotá.")

In the meantime, I was getting acquainted with the missionaries at Carmelo. Most of them were from Canada and were an exceptionally high caliber of missionaries in my opinion. However, it freaked them all out that we were going to live with the Indians. They felt that they had given up a lot to be willing to live at Carmelo and minister to the country Colombians. They had seen Santiago and other Indians and were impressed by their lack of cleanliness and strange customs. They didn't see how we were going to take our family of four children, including a handicapped baby, and live with them. They wanted to give us all the help they possibly could.

The Bible school students were also quite impressed. Sometimes they felt jealousy because the missionaries had wringer washing machines, tile floors, warm showers (by laying coils of hose on the roofs of their houses to heat in the sun), and other amenities that the country Colombians didn't have in their homes. The missionaries felt justified in their few conveniences and luxuries by pleading that they had left fine, well-equipped homes in Canada. Compared to those, their houses at Carmelo would seem like shacks. Of course the Colombians having never been to Canada couldn't appreciate the contrast. However, they knew how the Indians lived, and it blew these Colombian young people's minds that here was an American family going to live with the Indians in a much more primitive manner than they, the rural Colombians, experienced in their own homes. They too wanted to help us in any way possible.

The staff and students had just finished a two-month period of intensive prayer for the Indians. They realized that they had neither training nor time to reach these Kogis. The few who wanted to express their love and friendship tried to do it with a big bear hug, the Colombian *abrazo,* to overcome the language barrier. This did not have the desired effect on the Kogis who had very little physical contact with one another. They didn't even shake hands. This outward show of affection embarrassed and annoyed the Kogis. The

Colombian Christians, as well as the missionaries, were thrilled that trained specialists had arrived to tackle this problem in answer to their prayers. From our viewpoint, it was thrilling to be the answer to their prayers.

Every now and then, all the women missionaries at Carmelo had a sewing bee. We each took mending or handwork and met in someone's living room. This was a friendly time of interchange and gave me a chance to know each one better. The older missionaries told me that this time was very important. It kept them all friendly and kept them from gossiping about each other. (At least that was what I was told.) These get-togethers were held once or twice a month, I think. Another type of social activity for the missionaries took place in the evening and included the men too. This was a time for studying Spanish grammar. I didn't enjoy it much, as the grammar was all over my head. These missionaries were busy people. They taught classes in the Bible institute in the morning, and after the siesta in the afternoons, they were busy with the farming, lesson planning or other activities. They had many counseling sessions with the students, both men and women. Rules were strict, and romances were not tolerated during the six-month school session.

When the Bible institute was first started, the missionaries told me, they had a six-month session for men students, followed by a six-month session for women. This worked well, but it meant that the missionary staff had to teach year-round. Now they were experimenting with coeducation. This gave the missionary staff time for other activities, such as *cursillos*, short Bible courses, in the many churches that dotted the Department of Magdalena. Having the men and women together solved some problems, but of course it created others. One phenomenon that the missionaries related to us was that many of the girl students were prone to *ataques* (attacks). For no apparent reason one would start crying, screaming, and thrashing. Nothing could be done with her until the *ataque* ran its course. The missionaries had tried prayer, counseling, medications, visits to the doctor, even exorcism. But nothing seemed to have any effect in stopping or preventing the attacks. Once started, the girl had to just wear herself out. (Of course she was surrounded by concerned classmates and teachers during the course of the attack.) After a good rest, she would be her normal self. The staff did notice that two girls never had attacks at the same time.

These *ataques* were very disruptive to the smooth running of the Bible institute. Two or three times a week, someone would be having an attack. Finally as an experiment, a notice was posted. Girls could have one *ataque* per school semester. If anyone had more than one, she would be deemed too ill to study and be sent home. After the new ruling, several girls had one attack, but no one ever had the second one. After a while *ataques* seemed to go out of style.

When Sunday came, Chad was asked to speak in the church. I was embarrassed, afraid that he would make a lot of errors in Spanish, but no one else seemed to mind. Right after the service Gloria turned icy cold, in fact so cold that her face was blue, and she was shivering and shaking. No matter how many blankets I wrapped around her, she didn't warm up. Once again she wailed miserably like she had when first put into the cast. I gave her baby aspirin, but it didn't do any good. This continued for several hours, and then she broke into a sweat and spiked a fever. After that, she was just listless and pale. I couldn't figure out what was wrong with her. She was nine months old, and I thought she might be teething, but teething never had brought on symptoms like that in any of my other children. We went to bed, but I lay awake for many hours, puzzled about Gloria's strange illness. In the morning Chad planned to go back to Santiago's farm to see how our house was coming along.

Chapter 3

Magic Furniture

Carmelo
June 1965

In the grayness of the predawn morning, I decided that the sickness that had affected Gloria must be malaria. Since we had not counted on any of us coming down with that tropical disease in the cool mountain climate of the Sierra, we had not brought with us any anti-malarial medicines. I knew that early Monday morning the Carmelo jeep would take off for Santa Marta. I poked Chad and told him to hurry and catch the driver and order some malaria medicine. There would not be another opportunity until the following Monday. As Chad was pulling on his pants, we heard the jeep engine start. Before he had his shoes on, the jeep was starting up the long switchback that led to the town of San Pedro. Chad took off straight up the mountainside without the benefit of a trail. By superhuman effort (according to him) he reached the road as it went through San Pedro, straight up above the guesthouse just before the jeep did. He managed to stop the driver and order some malaria medicine.

Chad had made a maximum effort and felt that he had strained his heart. (There was a history of early heart attacks in his mother's side of the family, and he had always been warned by her to take care of his heart.) He lay down again to recuperate, thus delaying his start for Santiago's farm, and in a little while who should appear but Santiago himself. With him were Alfonso and two Kogi men from Don Diego, Santiago's home village.   One was a fairly tall Kogi, not especially interesting, but the other was a man past middle age, short, and wearing a white, pointed Mama's hat (*numptu* we learned it was called in Kogi). Santiago introduced him as Mama Simon, an important *mama* (chief) and a good friend of Santiago's.

I asked if they wanted breakfast, and their faces lit up. I made a big pot of oatmeal, and then asked them how they wanted their eggs. (This showed my ignorance of Kogis as later experience showed they would have been delighted however I served them.) My question caused quite a bit of confusion. I had to explain to Santiago that I could boil them, fry, or scramble them. After quite a bit of discussion in the Kogi language, Santiago told me in Spanish to boil them. He always spoke emphatically as if giving me orders.

I then asked if they wanted them hard- or soft-boiled. This again called for quite a bit of discussion. Finally Santiago responded that they had decided that hard-boiled would be best so they wouldn't get their hair messy. The answer puzzled me, but I hard-boiled their eggs while they ate their bowls of oatmeal and powdered milk. (In contrast to the non-Indian Colombians, who detest our kind of oatmeal, Kogis love the way North Americans make porridge from oatmeal and serve it with milk and sugar.) When I served the eggs, I understood why they wanted them hard-boiled. Each Kogi cracked his egg on his head, then peeled it and ate it. Yes, a soft-boiled egg might have gotten their hair messy. After they ate their eggs, they wiped their hands on their hair.

Chad had spent his time at Carmelo "prefabbing" some furniture to take unassembled to Santiago's place. Santiago agreed to come the next day with some oxen and carry the unassembled furniture back to our house. He told us the house was drying out nicely and that we could soon move in. Before dark the jeep arrived from Santa Marta with our malaria medicine. I can't remember what we gave to Gloria, but she has never had a malaria attack again, as far as I know, to this day.

The next morning, true to his word, Santiago arrived with two oxen and his wife, María Elena, as well as Alfonso. This was the first time I had seen a Kogi woman. Later on we thought María Elena was very beautiful, but this morning she looked quite grumpy and sullen. She was suffering from a piece of wild cane that had been embedded in her hand. Her whole arm ached, Santiago told us. We hoped we would be able to help her as soon as we got our medicine unpacked. The woman's clothes were quite interesting. A large piece of cotton cloth had been wrapped around her body and tied sarong style, leaving one shoulder bare. The oxen were huge animals. An exceptionally large white one belonged to Santiago. "Santiago's Magic Ox" we later called him. The other was a black creature loaned by another Kogi family. The oxen carried large Kogi-made jute carrying bags slung across their backs, sort of like huge motorcycle saddlebags. Chad and Alfonso filled them with the lumber that would later become our household furniture.

The next day Chad borrowed some of the Carmelo pack mules and a Bible school student or two to act as mule drivers and began to transport some of our belongings to our house. He would stay there long enough to assemble the furniture. He had made a kitchen table, a long worktable for one side of the kitchen, a crib, a triple bunk bed, a double bed, and a single bed for Alba, plus some benches of different sizes. We had light foam rubber mattresses for all these beds, plus lots of duffle bags with our personal possessions and household equipment. A briefcase contained our empty notebooks, 3x5 cards, and meager linguistic data. A new Olivetti portable typewriter (a real strain on our budget), and a small reel-to-reel Norelco tape recorder completed our linguistic equipment. We also had a battery-powered radio transmitter and receiver and antenna for keeping in touch with Lomalinda. All the things we didn't need at Carmelo were packed up and sent down the trail to our new house on Santiago's farm.

When Chad got to our new house and started putting together the furniture, he realized that there wasn't enough floor space in the house to set up all the beds. The house was quite small, and the floor space had been divided into two rooms by a mud wall. The larger room, Santiago told him, was the school. The other very small room in the back was for us all to sleep in. He probably thought we women and children would sleep on the ground and Chad would swing a hammock over the top of us, Kogi style.

For a while Chad was stumped, and then he got a bright idea. Santiago had come back from Bogotá with the impression that we were *very* tall. As a result he had built a *very* high roof. An off-centered pole divided what would be the ceiling into two sections and rested on the mud wall dividing the rooms and went through the house and out the ends where it also rested on the tops of the walls. The boards for the double bed just fit the larger side, and the boards for the bunk beds just fit the smaller side. He made an upstairs for the children and us out of the boards for the beds.   He then laid out our mattresses on the floor of the new upstairs. He put together the crib and the single bed in the small room on the main floor and made the larger room, "the school," into the kitchen.   The long worktable went along the end wall with a shelf below for pots and pans. The Coleman white gas stove would go on the middle of the counter (tabletop). A large box with a shelf and a curtain closure positioned on the left of the worktable would contain the medicine, while a similar box with a hinged door closure would be set to the right to hold the dishes. The hinged door would be closed at night, keeping the dishes bug and dust free. (All these tricks we had learned at Jungle Camp.) He placed benches along each wall except in the area of the table, and we had our kitchen and school combined. Santiago was very happy with the arrangement.   A long, notched tree trunk had been used as a ladder to thatch the roof. This was brought inside and would serve as the ladder to the loft.

The Kogis were amazed at the speed with which this furniture went together. The only pieces of furniture they possessed were little stools that they laboriously hacked and carved with a machete and an axe from pieces of tree trunks out in the jungle. Each one took a long time to make. How Chad could come up with an entire houseful of furniture in a few hours was a marvel to them.   "What else could this wonder worker do?" they thought.

Chapter 4

Our First Student

Upon our arrival at Santiago's place, the mules assembled in a small bare, level area on the far side of the new house. This was our front patio. We were home! The Kogis retreated to the security of Santiago's house, except for Santiago of course who was giving orders and directing things as much as possible.

The Colombians rapidly unloaded the mules. I felt I had to give them something to eat before they left, so I quickly made sandwiches from some sliced bread one of the missionary ladies had given me and some canned meat, something like Spam. With bananas and water to drink, the Colombian men mounted America and another mule and took off at a fast clip. The cargo mules fell in behind them. The first drops of rain had started as we came up the slope from the river. In another half hour or so, the downpour would start.

I was terribly tired, but this was no time to rest. I changed Gloria's diaper and made her a bottle, and then, giving her into Alba's care, I tackled the task of unpacking and making this little mud house livable.

Actually, Chad had done a wonderful preliminary job of setting us up. The children clambered up and down the notched pole, tying up their bags of personal items and arranging their sleeping bags on their foam rubber pads. I fixed up Gloria's crib, and when she went to sleep, Alba placed her in her new crib and arranged her own sleeping area.

After the Colombian men had departed, all of the Kogis came over to our house. Santiago started telling us about each one's ills. We found remedies to treat the worst cases but told most of them that they would have to wait until tomorrow when we had our medicines unpacked. I worked on the kitchen area, trying to arrange things in a workable manner, while Chad unpacked the medicines and first aid equipment. After a while I realized that Alba was sitting on a bench reading a book she had found, so I got her busy helping me unpack. It doesn't seem like much now, but at the time I was very angry with her. By her inattention to the duty at hand, I felt betrayed and deserted in my time of great need. We must have eaten something for supper, but I have no idea what. Finally it was time to go to bed. Gloria would have to sleep upstairs with the rest of us, but the crib below would be good for her daytime naps. The children scrambled up the ladder, but I presented a different problem. Every time I got about halfway up, the log swiveled, and I was dumped back down again. Finally with the children pulling from above, Chad gave a mighty heave from below, and I was up. The next day he drove large spikes in the notches to make the footholds more secure.

We had only brought one mosquito net to protect the baby. Since we were well above the malaria zone, we decided not to bother with nets for the rest of us. We all felt snug in our sleeping bags as we settled down for our first night in the tribal area. Chad led us all in a prayer of thanksgiving for our safe trip over the trail. Just as we were dozing off to sleep, a searing pain struck me in the left shoulder. I thought of snakebite, but it turned out to be some kind of a wasp with a huge stinger. Chad removed the stinger by flashlight and applied alcohol to the sting, but it hurt for a long time. I felt that dark forces were giving us notice that they were not yet defeated. The fight was just beginning.

The next morning after our arrival at Santiago's farm, the first thing we had to face was the water problem. María Elena had brought us a five-gallon can full of water the night before. We had made oatmeal for breakfast and washed the dishes, and the water was gone. I had a large plastic bag of dirty diapers plus all the other dirty clothes from the trip over the trail. Santiago had made it clear to Chad that men were not allowed to carry water. Water carrying was a woman's job in the Kogi tribe. Men brought firewood. It was okay for Chaddy and Russell to bring water as they were not yet men, Santiago told us. We sent them down to the river with buckets, but the water slopped all over them on the steep uphill trail, and their clean jeans were plastered with mud. The little bit of water left in their pails wouldn't even wash their jeans.

We sent them back with the five-gallon can with a corncob plug. Full, it was too heavy for them, but they came back with a little more water this time. The boys were eight and nine by now. They could do a lot of things, but they were not going to make very good water carriers. We sent Alba down with a great big cooking kettle that belonged to Santiago. While chasing Chaddy back up the hill, she banged the kettle against a rock and made a small dent. That happening evoked the ire of Santiago, "You great big senorita," he hollered. "Why aren't you married instead of running around and playing with the kids?"

I took the bag of diapers to the river, but my rubber flip flops sunk into the muddy trail and were never found again. Santiago sent María Elena to help me with the diapers, but she told Santiago she would never do that again. "She washes clothes that aren't even dirty," María Elena told Santiago. I later found that the Kogi women just dry the rags they use for diapers and use them many times before washing them.

Even though the diapers were now clean, I still had the huge pile of all of our travel clothes to be washed. I didn't know how I was going to handle that chore.

Meanwhile Chad had set up the tribal radio and antenna and called Lomalinda. They wanted to know the name of our tribal location. I asked Santiago what we should call his place, and after a bit of consultation with María Elena, they named their farm San Antonio. Chad also unpacked a large heavy canvas container to hold water. It was called a Lister bag. He had bought it in an army surplus store. This hung from a rafter and had spigots on all sides, for army personnel to use to wash their hands, etc. If we only could get that filled, we would have water for several days. We had a small hand-powered washing machine that we had ordered from Missionary Equipment Services in Chicago. It had a hand-powered plunger on one end and a wringer, also hand powered, on the other. We had also brought a large plastic container to use for rinsing, but how were we to get the water from the river far below? Santiago wrinkled his brow, trying to solve this unforeseen dilemma. A Kogi family used very little water. He thought his five-gallon can full of water would be ample.

All the Kogis who lived in the neighborhood had come to see us again. Chad was busy treating their ailments. Each one brought us a gift of bananas, yuca, plantains, malanga or arracacha. These last two were root vegetables that formed a staple of the Kogi diet. We later found out that our visitors had to stop at Santiago's house first and show him their gift. If he thought it was good enough, he sent them up. I heated some water and seated María Elena on a bench with her injured hand in a container of warm water. I also started her on a treatment with sulfa pills. I was hoping that if we could control the infection, we might be able to get the large splinter out. She was happy to sit in the kitchen and interpret for me as I treated the other Kogis. She, as well as Santiago, knew quite a bit of Spanish. Most of the people had large abdomens, which indicated parasite infestation. Chad started them all on a two-day treatment of worm medicine. It was sticky syrup, and they all loved it. Some needed treatment for diarrhea. Many had respiratory infections. Alfonso's grandfather, Jose Sundungama, needed treatment for his arthritis. He was the unfriendliest of the whole bunch, so Chad really wanted to do a good job on him. He gave him a vitamin B-complex shot, a course of aspirin treatment, and some multivitamins.

By the time we were finished with all the treatment, it was lunchtime. Alba had made a big kettle of rice, and I made creamed tuna to go on top. We must have had something else too, but I don't remember what. We finished it all off with chocolate pudding. I invited all the Indians who were around to eat with us. I could tell I had done the right thing. Their expressions changed from scowls to smiles.

After lunch the Kogis all went home. Soon the daily deluge started. We had to shut the doors and nail plastic over the windows to keep out the driving rain. It was too dark to read, or to do much else, so we all climbed back to our beds for our afternoon siesta. We were happy to note that our cleverly woven thatched roof did not leak. We had set out pails to catch rain water off the eaves but were very disappointed to find it was a dark yellow color from the thatch; we couldn't even use it to wash the dirty clothes. After the rain was over, Santiago came to visit us with Alfonso in tow. Alfonso was going to stay with us, Santiago announced. He could sleep at Santiago's house, but we had to feed him. We readily agreed. We assumed that he was there to help us and especially to carry water. He was older and stronger than Russell and Chaddy but was not yet considered to be an adult man, so he could still carry water. Chad gave him the five-gallon can and indicated that he wanted the Lister bag filled. Alfonso shook his head, no. Chad offered him some pesos, but Alfonso still shook his head. Money was no good to him when there were no stores around. Then Chad got a bright idea. He showed him some bubblegum. Alfonso nodded his head.

Alfonso placed the five-gallon can in a large Kogi mochila and swung it onto his back with the long strap supported by his forehead. He had been carrying heavy loads in this manner since he was very young, and his neck muscles were strong. He also picked up the large kettle, which he would carry in his hands. After several trips, the Lister bag was full. I tried to tell him that was enough, but he went back to the river and arrived with another load. I filled the dishpans, the tea kettle, and the washing machine. Still he went back for more water. I filled the rinse tub, all the buckets, and the cooking kettles. Finally there was not another container in which to pour water. When I couldn't empty the containers anymore, Alfonso took the full containers back to Santiago. We all had water for several days.

The next day Santiago asked us if we were not even going to give Alfonso a notebook and a pencil. Now we understood that he was there to study. Santiago had built a school, and Alfonso was the pupil. He was the only teenaged boy among Santiago's neighbors. We found out that Alfonso had been Santiago's brother-in-law. Alfonso's sister who had been Santiago's wife had drowned in the river about a year or so before Chad's first meeting with Santiago. Santiago had really loved this woman and still had a close relationship with her family. Alfonso knew only a few words of Spanish, but he had already made friends with our children at Lomalinda when he had been there for the first linguistic workshop a few months previously. Every day I tried to teach him some written words. Since I didn't know his language, and he didn't know mine, I used words that were quite uncomplicated to write. I started with *mama*. This was what the Kogis called their leaders. When he could write that, I tried other words such as *hui*, house; *misi*, cat; *piu,* dog; and *bakka*, cow. He could copy the words just fine, but he couldn't remember which one was which. I tried numbers and found that math was much more meaningful to him.

He soon knew all the numbers to ten and could do simple addition and subtraction. Meanwhile we were all using a mixture of English, Spanish, and Kogi and communicating however we could.

During our first days in the tribe, we had a visit from our nearest Spanish-speaking neighbors, Luis and Josefina. They lived about half an hour's hike away on a ridge that could be seen from our house. Luis had been a policeman in Bogotá and had come to the Sierra to start a coffee farm. Their rapidly growing family needed a school, and they had been delighted when Santiago announced that he was building one. They were disappointed to hear that we were not planning to open an elementary school for Spanish-speaking children. However, they remained very good and friendly neighbors. The Colombian people were always amazed that Santiago had built our house on a ridge where there were no streams higher up that could be channeled to our house by bamboo canals or rubber tubing. The church at Carmelo wanted to take up an offering to buy tubing to bring water to our house. Several of the men visited us to plan the project, but they concluded that it was not possible. There was just no water available to pipe to our house.

We soon found that none of the Kogis would speak to us in the Kogi language. Santiago would sit down and have a formal session of language study once a day in accordance with his agreement with Chad, but in common, everyday matters, he stuck to Spanish. So did María Elena. They still remembered that there was a death threat against anyone who taught an outsider their language. They gave us simple words for objects when we asked, but everything else was very complicated. Santiago would not allow us to communicate in Kogi "baby talk." We had to use long perfect Kogi utterances, or communicate in Spanish. Alfonso was learning Spanish much faster than we were learning Kogi. Somehow, in spite of the language barrier, we were all able to get along and soon felt like a family.

One of Gloria's few toys in our tribal location was a small clown doll. Usually she was frightened of clowns, but this one was unique. He was covered with soft white terry cloth and wore a pointed hat. His body and limbs were round and chubby. Santiago called him Mama Nacio and liked to make him dance. This broke up the other Kogis into gales of laughter. They finally told us that Mama Ignacio (Mama Nacio) was the shaman of Mamarongo, the most respected and famous leader on the western side of the mountains. He was noted for being plump, quite unusual in a Kogi, especially a mama, and he always wore a pointed white hat. Often, when a group gathered, Santiago picked up the doll and started moving him in the deliberate steps and rhythm of a Kogi dance. Invariably even the most sober-faced Kogi started laughing.

In spite of their amusement with the doll, we soon found out that the Kogis in our area did not like the Kogis in the village of Mamarongo. Santiago and his neighbors had their roots in the village of Don Diego to the north. We were to find that there were feuds and bad relations among the different villages and families. Santiago was determined that if we were going to move to a village, it was going to be Don Diego.

During this, our first stay at Santiago's farm, we were visited by a team from Gospel Recordings. This is a mission that is also called to work with all the unreached language groups in the world. Their mission and methods are a little different from that of Wycliffe. They come with recording equipment. Working through a bilingual, they record short Bible stories and gospel messages in the native languages. Santiago was the ideal bilingual for this type of work. The messages can

then be played on a tape player, or on ingenious hand-powered phonographs. They recorded about six messages in Kogi. These would be returned to us in the form of small phonograph records. In the meantime, Chad had recorded them on his reel-to-reel Norelco tape recorder (contrary to accepted Gospel Recordings procedures, we later discovered).

Chapter 5

A Close Call

I soon noticed that our food supply was diminishing rapidly. Santiago had recited a long list of items that were supposedly available in Kogiland. But I found that in actuality, most of them were seasonal or in short supply. For instance, take chickens and eggs. Every family owned a small flock of chickens; however, they rarely ate either chickens or eggs. They kept the eggs to hatch more chickens, and they kept the hens to lay more eggs. In the meantime, the small wild animals like foxes and weasels made off with both.

Visitors brought us abundant supplies of malanga, arracatcha, and all kinds of bananas, but it seemed like we could only eat so much of that kind of food. I had brought with us lots of oatmeal, some rice and some flour. I also had plenty of powdered milk for Gloria and our other children. A very special gift from the Kogis would be two eggs wrapped in a rag or tied up in dried cornstalks. Two eggs meant pancakes for breakfast and a chocolate cake for supper. Our supply of cooking oil dwindled rapidly as did our sugar and rice. Santiago solved the sugar problem by squeezing sugarcane and making brown sugar blocks, *panela.*

We found that this item was a staple in rural Colombia and provided a cash crop for the Kogis. Certain Kogi men were skilled in hacking and carving the rollers for the sugarcane press where the heavy logs lay out in the jungle. Then the rollers were dragged to the desired spot by humans or oxen and arranged in a very ingenious manner.   Three rollers were set up in a vertical position.   Cogs at the top enabled the side rollers to turn, powered by the middle roller. The middle roller was activated by an ox or burro going around in a circle.   A medium-sized boy drove the animal by running behind it with a stick, and an older teenager or an adult Kogi risked his hands and arms feeding the sugarcane between the rollers. In case of a mishap there was no "quick release switch."   Later, we were to realize the toll in one-armed Kogis that these primitive *trapiches* had extracted in spite of their ingenious construction.   The sugarcane juice was caught in a large iron caldron and boiled over a fire to the "hard ball stage."   Santiago and María Elena knew exactly when to remove the caldron from the fire.   To my amazement, at that point Santiago removed the door of his house, assembled some wooden slats on top of it, and there was his mold for the brown sugar blocks.   María Elena had been stirring the mixture all the while with a large paddle. At just the right point, two small paddles were used to scoop the hardening mass into the molds on top of the door, which now lay on the ground.   In an hour or so the mold was dismantled, the brown sugar blocks packed into a mochila to be sold, and Santiago's door was put back on his house.

We found the brown sugar to be delicious.   Santiago's *panela* was dark in color and free of additives.   Purchased *panela* we later found contained added chemicals to lighten the color and harden the blocks.   We preferred Santiago's homemade variety.   I learned to substitute shaved *panela* for at least half of the sugar in most recipes.   I also learned that I could reduce the oil by half as well without making much difference in the recipe.   I had brought a very large plastic bag of dehydrated potato slices.   It came with us from Minnesota, and I am not at all sure how we got it.   We used this entire bag during our first two months in the tribe.   It was a welcome change from the Kogi root vegetables. Once in a while a Kogi woman brought me a few stalks of long green onions. This also was a great gift. Santiago instructed me to sniff the onions repeatedly and make a "big deal" of such a gift. Potatoes and onions were grown in the *Páramo*, the high mountain country above the tree line. Once in a while a Kogi brought us a few small round potatoes that he had carried down from the *Páramo* in his mochila. Basically we were told that if we wanted to eat beef, potatoes, and onions, we had to go to the *Páramo*.

Once in a while a Kogi family would come with a young rooster. This meant that we had to kill and clean it, and the whole Kogi family would stay for dinner. Santiago informed me that the muscular parts of the chicken, especially the breast (my favorite part) could only be eaten by the men. The women got the head, feet, and intestines. That was one time that I told him we would eat chicken according to our customs, not his. We soon found that María Elena was willing to kill and clean the chicken for us in exchange for the "women's portions." Since Chad and most of the children preferred the dark meat, I would take a very small piece of the breast and divide the rest with Santiago and any men present. The women were content to share María Elena's portion. We learned to not waste ANYTHING. Alba gave some leftover oatmeal porridge one morning to Santiago's tiny, skinny black dog. Soon Santiago showed up in the kitchen to report on her grievous crime. No food whatsoever was to be given to the dog. If we started feeding him, Santiago gravely pointed out, the dog would no longer perform his function in life. Santiago promised to show up midmorning every day for a coffee break and personally take care of any breakfast leftovers.

One Saturday morning Alba told us sadly that life was too difficult at San Antonio, and she wanted to return to Bogotá. "The life of you missionaries is too hard for me," she said. Chad told her that he couldn't personally take her back to Bogotá, but that on Sunday he would take her to Carmelo to go down to Santa Marta in the jeep on Monday. She would have to take the train back to Bogotá. We had been trying to make Alba go to bed when we did. She would sit up late reading by candlelight. We were afraid she would ruin her eyes, and she was rapidly using up our small supply of candles. However, that Saturday night, seeing that she was sad and homesick, we let her read to her heart's content. On Sunday morning she told us she had changed her mind. She had read the story of Gideon in the Bible and decided she didn't want to be like one of the men who went home. She would stay with us and be like one of the brave 300 who won the victory. Further developments proved that she made the right decision. Alba was not much of a "maid" and I did not expect her to be one. She was more like a "mother's helper" or a visiting cousin who helped out with household tasks. I didn't demand much of her, and she had a lot of free time to read or play with the kids. But in a few days we would really need her help.

Just when our outside food supply got really low, corn on the cob came into season. It was not sweet corn, but regular field corn picked when young and tender. To us it was delicious. Our family could practically live on corn on the cob. The mission station, Carmelo, had a mission chapel at a place about two hours beyond us on the trail. On alternate weekends Carmelo students or one of the missionary men made the trip by mule to preach at the chapel, and they always stopped to rest at our house, bringing us our mail, and often several pounds of beef. This was a very welcome addition to our diet, although it had to be eaten within a day or two as we had no refrigeration and no fire over which to smoke it.

One phenomenon was causing us quite a bit of trouble. Ever since we arrived at Santiago's farm, we all had to get up frequently to go to the bathroom at night. Sometimes it was four times apiece for Chad and me, and traffic was heavy on the notched pole. Chad had dug a posthole some distance away from the house, and rigged up some kind of semi-private shelter around it, but it was annoying to have to make so many trips out there in the middle of the night. At last in desperation we dedicated our largest galvanized bucket to sanitary duty. We placed it under a folding toilet seat, designed to be used with plastic bags in boats. (This had been a gift from someone in Minnesota.) We placed a strong solution of pine oil disinfectant in the bottom, and we had our indoor toilet. We rigged up this makeshift bathroom just in the nick of time.

One morning, a week or so after Alba had decided to stay with us, I woke up not feeling well. In fact I felt terrible. I had chills. I ached all over and had an intense pain in my back. Chad diagnosed a kidney infection, dosed me with aspirin and antibiotic, and ordered me to bed rest. After several hours I spiked a fever and broke into a sweat. I felt better but terribly weak. (That is why it was great that we had indoor bathroom facilities. I could never have made it down the pole, out to the posthole, and back up again.) I lay weakly on my stomach on my mattress on the floor of our loft, looking down at all that went on in the kitchen. It was not a pleasant drama. Now Alba had all the work to do by herself. To Chad she was the maid and was supposed to do the cooking, take care of Gloria, change dirty diapers, etc. She rebelled. I tried to direct from my vantage point upstairs. To the children, I was Mama looking down from the sky. Most of the time, Gloria was left in bed with me. The children helped with the work, but they were still too little to do it all. It was a blessing we still had Alba, who, when she realized how sick I was, really tried to do her best.

Towards night I had another bout of chills and intense pain in the back. The antibiotic and aspirin didn't seem to do much good. The evening attack was worse than the one in the morning had been. Before midnight I was into the sweating and fever again. By morning, I couldn't even sit on the bucket. Chad had to hold me up. I knew that I had never been so sick before in my life. I wished that the antibiotic would take a hold. Because of the chills and back pain, coupled with the frequent urination, I had no doubts that the illness was a kidney infection. Chad called the nurse at Lomalinda on the radio and was told that he was taking the right course of treatment. The only problem was that it didn't seem to be working. Gloria was still left in bed with me, but I couldn't take care of her anymore. I couldn't even change her diaper. I began to wonder if I was going to die right there under that thatched roof. I wondered what would become of the children, especially Gloria. I had read of Indian tribes who buried babies alive with the mother should she die. For the first time I could understand this custom. Who would take care of Gloria if I didn't make it? I started considering each one of the single ladies in our Wycliffe branch. In the afternoon another round of chills and pain hit me. No amount of blankets could make me warm. The pain in my back was close to insupportable. Each attack was worse than the one before. I had not been able to eat since the start of this illness. Now I could hardly sip liquid. I felt that I could not survive another of these intense and ever-worsening attacks. I was almost beyond being able to think. Chad was still bringing me the antibiotic and aspirin on schedule, but I could hardly swallow the pills, and they didn't seem to be doing any good.

Chad was spending all his time reading the medical book, trying to diagnose what was wrong with me. He considered malaria, but dismissed it as the cycle was supposed to be 24 or 48 hours. My attacks were occurring somewhere between six and twelve hours apart. Now I was in the fever and weakness stage. I was really weak. I couldn't even talk above a whisper. I let my hand hang over the edge and wiggled a finger if I needed help. I have no idea what the children and Alba were thinking, but Chad was desperate. He lit the Coleman lantern and stayed up all night praying and reading the medical book. I had whispered to him that I couldn't survive another cycle and had whispered the name of the person I thought would be the best for him to marry and have help him raise the kids. I guess that really scared him.

Sometime between midnight and dawn, he climbed the pole with an injection syringe. He mumbled something about the fact that we couldn't ignore the possibility of malaria and injected me. I went to sleep and woke up better in the morning. My recovery took a while, but I didn't have another of those painful chills. It took about a week before I could resume some of my former duties, and by that time we had to think about packing up and taking the children back to school at Lomalinda.

The missionaries at Carmelo sent the mules on the prearranged day. As America climbed the steep mountain switchbacks with me on her back, I looked down at the little thatched roof that still stood out like a yellow haystack against the brown and green terrain. How close I came to dying under that yellow thatched roof, I remembered. How many women live, give birth, and die under those little thatched roofs, I thought. I gave thanks for America, the strong mule, who was taking me back to that other world that I had almost forgotten existed, where water came out of faucets, toilets flushed, food could be purchased at a grocery store, doctors could be called, and ambulances rushed the sick to a hospital.

I thought back to the illness that Gloria had suffered in Carmelo. Had it not been for Chad's early morning run up the hill to catch the Carmelo jeep and order the malaria medicine, I may not have been sitting in the saddle at that moment. I remembered Russell's words that terrible evening before Chad gave me the malaria injection. "We can't just let Mother die here," I heard him say to Chad. "Can't we call for a mule from Carmelo?"

"But Mother is too sick. She can't sit on a mule," Chad replied. "Can't we tie her on with her head hanging over one side, and her feet over the other?" Russell wondered.

Hearing this exchange, I had thought to myself, "I had better die right here in my bed rather than start out on a trip like that."

Although still very weak, at least I could now sit in the saddle. I gave thanks to the Lord who had brought me through this close call. I determined that I would do all I could for other women, and men too, who lived in those little thatched-roofed houses and had little or no hope neither in this life nor in the world to come.

Chapter 6

Social Graces or
the Lack of Them

Carmelo, Bogotá, August 1965

The missionaries at Carmelo were kind of surprised to see us back so soon. I guess they thought we were going to stay permanently at Santiago's farm. When we explained that we had to take the children back to school at Lomalinda, they wondered why we didn't put them in school at Carmelo instead. In a few weeks the missionary children would be arriving from all over northern Colombia for the new school year. Some mentioned that a German family had just vacated a large house on the far side of San Pedro. They thought we should rent it, put our children in school at Carmelo, and we could still make trips to stay for a few days at a time at Santiago's house. It was a tempting idea, but Uncle Cam Townsend would not agree to it. It was not the Wycliffe way. We were to spend several months living among the people gathering data, then return to Lomalinda where we could receive help in the analysis from the linguistic specialists. We loaded our duffle bags onto the Carmelo jeep, and down we went to Santa Marta again.

No one was happier than Alba to be back to civilization. We bought her an airplane ticket so she could fly with us back to Bogotá. She was really looking forward to being with her family again. To my surprise, about two hours after we had arrived at the Bogotá Group House, I received a call from Alba. She wanted to go back to Lomalinda with us. Somehow I just couldn't face taking her on again. I felt that she should stay with her family. She would soon be 17 and could start her studies at the Bible institute.

After settling the three older children in school, we returned to our tribal location again. Wycliffe ran a very fine children's home at Lomalinda where the kids could live while their parents went to the tribe. Our departure was saddened by Sharon coming down with malaria. She was too sick to stay in the children's home, but our very good neighbor Edna Hedland offered to take her into her home until she recovered. This whole trip to the tribe was a sad one for me as everywhere were reminders of our three school-aged children left behind at Lomalinda. We had given some of the children's clothes that they were outgrowing to Luis and Josefina's family, our nearest Colombian neighbors. Evidently, one of Sharon's colorful dresses must have been too worn out for much use, and they had torn it into small lengths to be braided into the girls' hair like ribbons. This dress had a sentimental history, as Chad had fought with a bunch of women at a bargain counter to buy it when Sharon was only one year old. It was a huge dress for Sharon at the time, and I had carefully kept it until it was the right size. Now I was overcome with nostalgia as I saw discarded strips of the distinctive print along the trail as we neared our little house. I realized that this separation was only for a short time. I remembered that missionaries in China and India had been separated from their school-aged children for many years at a time. At least Wycliffe was very considerate about keeping families together as much as possible.

Santiago told us that he had had visitors from the village of Mamarongo three days to the south. A message had come from the leadership of the village. It was for Chad. "If you or any of the Kogis under your influence come here, you will be killed."

Santiago was not intimidated. He wanted to go right down there and tell them a thing or two. "Aren't you afraid?" someone asked him.

"Oh, no, Chad will go with me," was Santiago's reply.

Wisdom prevailed. "We will wait for God to open the door," Chad told him. And to me he said, "We can't just go over there and kick the door in."

I remember little about that stay in the tribe, except that I was able to organize the myriads of 3x5 cards on which Chad had collected Kogi words. I believe this was also the time Santiago almost died of poisoning. This story is told in *High Adventure in Colombia.*

With the lack of access to water in their homes, the only water being the cold, cold streams flowing right from the snow-capped peaks usually located down a steep muddy trail from their homes, we soon realized that the Kogis were not frequent bathers. In fact, I observed that Santiago and María Elena, who were among the cleaner ones, averaged a bath and change of clothes about once every two weeks. The women with babies became especially odoriferous as their garment became frequently saturated with baby urine or worse. The babies were wrapped in old clothes or pieces of hammocks. When wet, the wrappings were thrown over the side of the house to dry. Fecal material was wiped off with a dry plantain peel. Once in a while the mother gathered up all these evil-smelling rags and washed them in the river. One day as we were just finishing breakfast, some visitors arrived. Chad arranged some benches for them to sit on not far from the table. All of a sudden, Santiago turned to me and asked if I had an extra bar of soap. I got him one out of our supply barrel. Taking the soap he turned to the visiting woman and said, "Here, take this soap and go wash yourself and your baby and everything you have on. Patricia is going to throw up her breakfast if she has to sit there and smell you." I was terribly embarrassed for the poor woman, but she was delighted with the gift of soap and did as she was told. The next time we came to the tribe, I brought several extra boxes of soap, some the blue bars for washing clothes, and some small brightly colored bars that smelled wonderful for bathing. Everyone got a bar of each kind on their first visit, and after that our visitors looked clean and smelled much better.

We finished our linguistic goals and headed back to Lomalinda to be with our children for Christmas, our comings and goings a constant source of amazement to our missionary friends in Carmelo and Santa Marta.

In Bogotá we found that many new missionaries had arrived. They would be starting Spanish study at the end of January as we had done the year before. It was fun to get to know these new friends and coworkers, many of whom would soon be like family to us in time to come. Of course they looked up to us as experienced missionaries right fresh from our tribal assignment, the goal they had been looking forward to during so many years of preparation.

Each one of these new families had a distinctive story to tell of the Lord's dealings in their lives and the path that led them to Colombia. I found that there were many different roads to the mission field and many different reasons that these folks had arrived in Colombia. I sort of organized them in my mind into three different classes -- one being those who had been raised by their families to be missionaries. Perhaps they were second- or third-generation full-time Christian workers. From childhood they had been brought up to know that they were expected to go to a foreign field. (In many churches in the '50s and '60s missionaries had the highest status in the Christian community. Even my mother back in Minneapolis unexpectedly enjoyed being included in the elite group of "mothers of missionaries.")

These people who had been raised to be missionaries usually went to a Christian college or Bible institute and found a like-minded mate either during college or later at SIL or Jungle Camp. Now they were here to fulfill not only their own dreams, but also those of a solid devoted family and church constituency back home. They usually had good financial support, and lots of barrels lovingly packed with all the things they could possibly need for four or five years in Colombia.

The second group had sort of come in through the back door—their love for and talent in linguistics. They usually had a solid secular education in linguistics and had perhaps married someone from the first group along the way. What better way to get immersed into an unwritten language and gather material for a doctor's degree than to join the Wycliffe Bible Translators/Summer Institute of Linguistics. These people usually completed the analysis of their assigned language quite rapidly, being more interested in the linguistics than anything else, and then became our consultants and other linguistic leaders.

Then there were ones like Chad and me who had come from a different career, not especially loving linguistics, but seeing it as a necessary, tiresome task to enable us to communicate with primitive people. Perhaps I could also say those with a strong call of God on their lives, and a driving love for the souls of the unreached Indians. Of course there was a great deal of blending back and forth among these three basic types.

One night I sat visiting with a bubbly, new missionary wife and mother who I would classify as one of the first types. The road to the mission field for most people is always longer than expected. She and her husband had experienced several delays, but now here they were, actually in Colombia, with two small boys in tow. Fresh from Santiago's farm, I listened as she recounted how she and her husband didn't want to turn into dowdy, backwoods missionaries. She wanted her boys to grow up to be gentlemen in every sense of the word. She confided that they had their home at Lomalinda all planned to be an example of gracious living, and the money in hand to make their dream come true. Also, she told me that she had brought nice dishes, including crystal goblets,

so that her sons would be raised with every social amenity and would be able to fit right into polite society back home. I can't even express how deeply this conversation distressed me. I had sold most of our nice things, including sterling silver and crystal goblets, to pay for our tickets to Colombia. I was willing to use enameled ware and cheap stainless steel tableware like the country people of Colombia. Was I consigning our children to be country bumpkins, devoid of any social graces?

I could not dwell on this problem for long, as that night Gloria developed a raging fever. The local pediatrician who had diagnosed her hip problem made a midnight house call, applied an injection, and by morning she was better.

Chapter 7

Quarantined

Lomalinda and Villavicencio

As the small Helio Courier circled for a landing at Lomalinda, I saw through the window several small figures racing to the airstrip. Russell, Chaddy, and Sharon, accompanied by some of their friends, were coming to welcome us home. My mother's heart rejoiced to see my children again. I was comforted by the knowledge that they were right where they were supposed to be, running unfettered in the wide open spaces of the rolling hills of Lomalinda. Soon we were all together again. The children were strong and healthy, and their sun-bleached hair contrasted nicely with their tanned faces.

We had visited Gloria's doctor again in Bogotá, and he had changed her from the pillow splint to a brace. The brace held her left leg up in the air so no weight would be placed on her left femur. A built-up shoe on her right foot was supposed to compensate for the extra height of her left foot being up off the ground. Theoretically, she was supposed to be able to walk with this arrangement, but she never did. It was too hard to balance. It was sort of like walking on stilts, and she was only 15 months old and had never walked yet.

We were still in the little temporary cabin, but plans had been made for the construction of our permanent house,

and permission had been granted. Each man was allowed several weeks off from other duties to work on their house, and after Christmas Chad started on this project. It was fun finalizing our plans and picking out the colored cement tile for the different rooms. We would be one of the few families with an upstairs. Chad was able to put his experience in construction and engineering design to work, and the result was one of the largest houses, one of the most inexpensive to build, and one of the coolest. Chad oriented it so the hot midday sun never touched the long walls. Ventilation blocks shaded the southern side and also gave protection from the prevailing winds and storms. On the first floor were three bedrooms, a small study attached to our bedroom, a large kitchen, dining area, and living room. A cement tile walkway circled the house. Two bathrooms, one with an outside entrance for muddy children, and the other with a sunken shower that could be filled as a bathtub, served our needs. A small house off to one side would house Santiago or any Kogis who came to help us. Right down the middle of the house was a long narrow room designed to hold our storage barrels, and above this was a long upstairs room that would serve as the boys' sleeping loft. At the beginning, the loft was reached by a ladder, but later a full-sized stairway turned it into an accessible upstairs. We were very pleased with our plans and could hardly wait until our house would be a reality.

Looking at our water tower made of stacked-up barrels outside our little one-room temporary cabin, I realized that the clothes in those barrels would probably fit some of the children now, but there was no way to get to them without dismantling our entire water system. Chad said we would have to wait until our new house was ready. Then we would move everything over there and get into our barrels.

While Chad was building our house, I worked as much as possible on our linguistic analysis. The Kogi language just didn't come together neatly like the languages we had worked on at the university had done. It was like doing a jigsaw puzzle with some of the pieces missing and a few pieces left over that didn't fit anywhere. Chad decided to make a quick trip to the Sierra to bring back Alfonso to help with the language.

It was while Chad was at our tribal house by himself for a few days on this trip that the news came to him that Mama Nacio was dying in Mamarongo. All the important Kogi mamas from the eastern side of the mountains had gone to minister to him, but he had been getting steadily worse for ten months. Santiago went to visit him in spite of the death threat against any Kogi who had been influenced by us and found him indeed, very ill. He no longer resembled the chubby doll. He was skin and bones. He consented to let Chad come to minister to him. Chad knew that if he went and attempted to cure the mama and failed, he would not get out of that valley alive. This story is told in detail in *High Adventure in Colombia.* The Lord miraculously healed Mama Nacio and Chad played the Gospel Recordings for him and later for all the assembled village of Mamarongo. After talking it over, Santiago and Mama Nacio agreed that the gospel story told on those tapes was the truth and that Chad could continue to visit the village. This whole trip, though of immense importance to the future of our missionary work, and the Kogi tribe, took only about a week, and soon Chad was back at Lomalinda again with Alfonso.

I was surprised to see how much Alfonso had grown since we saw him last. He was very happy to return to Lomalinda with Chad. He felt like a brother to Chaddy and Russell, and he enjoyed our style of cooking. Some translators found that their Indian language helper had problems adjusting to their food. That was never a problem with any of the Kogis, just as long as there was enough of it. But Chad and I were disturbed to notice that after a few days of being with us again, there was a change in Alfonso's behavior. His smile was gone, and he seemed to have lost his appetite. Instead of playing with the boys, he just wanted to sit in the semi-dark lean-to. He made non-committal sounds when Chad

asked him what was wrong. Finally Chad figured it out.
Alfonso had a toothache. I don't remember how we got
the offending tooth extracted, but after a few days of painful
recovery, Alfonso was his old self again.

Soon it was time for another linguistic workshop. Santiago
and María Elena joined us. There were nine around our little
table. Chad built another lean-to on the other side of the
house. Now we had three lean-tos, one on every side except
for the front. The tape recorder sat on a shelf right above
Gloria's crib. We recorded the Kogis talking their language
and played it as much as possible. We suspected that maybe
the language was seeping into Gloria's subconscious baby
brain as she napped. It didn't seem to be penetrating our
thirty-something brains.

Santiago was quite free to talk about Kogi customs,
especially when he was far from the tribal area. When
someone remarked about how much Alfonso had grown,
Santiago mentioned that he was old enough to be initiated
into manhood now. A year ago Santiago had told us

Alfonso was 15. He had also told us that the Kogi initiation took place at age 20. I argued with him that Alfonso was only sixteen now and had four more years to go before he would be 20. I thought my logic was airtight, but Santiago wouldn't have it. I knew that the initiation involved coca use and sexual initiation. I wanted to stave that off for Alfonso and put it as far into the future as possible. "Well, no one can go from 15 to 20 in one year," I insisted.

"We can," replied Santiago. "It's a custom with us."

Chad's free time to work on the house had expired, so he hired a Colombian carpenter. After about a week, the carpenter said he needed a helper. Chad went over to the construction site unexpectedly one day and found the carpenter sitting in the shade under a tree drinking lemonade, and the helper doing a slipshod job of the carpentry work. Chad decided he wasn't going to pay one and a half times the salary of a carpenter to get inferior work done. The carpenter got fired, and Chad together with Russell and the Kogis worked on the house on weekends and after linguistic hours. Russell and Alfonso turned out to be quite good carpenters, and this was their start. I think Chaddy got involved as well.

The workshop ended, and the Kogis went back to the Sierra. I took Gloria to the doctor in Bogotá. When we arrived in Villavicencio on our way back to Lomalinda, I found Russell waiting for me at the airstrip. A note from the Lomalinda nurse said that she thought Russell had hepatitis. His skin and eyes were very yellow. Since I was going to be in Villavicencio, she had sent Russell to be seen by a doctor. We could return to Lomalinda on a flight the next day. We took a taxi to town and found a doctor.

"Yes, he has a little hepatitis," the Colombian doctor told me. "Put him on a low-fat and low-protein diet." And to Russell he said, "Be sure you eat a lot of candy."

Americans, especially nurses, have a healthy respect for this disease, but in Colombia, it was considered commonplace and no big deal. Russell had been very sick at Lomalinda with fever and nausea, but once he turned yellow, he seemed to feel better. Since this disease is an infection of the liver, American treatment is six weeks of bed rest on a high-carbohydrate, low-protein diet. I bought Russell some candy and found a cheap hotel for the night. Russell felt fine, but I made him stay in bed. He was very bored and wanted something to read. I put Gloria in her stroller and went out to look for some English reading material suitable for a nine-year-old boy. After trying several drug stores and newsstands, I found a large bookstore; however, my request for a children's book in English brought no results. Gloria and I were ambling along on the sidewalk, and I was trying to think of another store to try when two employees of the bookstore came running after us.

"We found one! We found one!" they called in Spanish. I waited for them, and they were very excited about having found a book for Russell. Then I looked at it. It was a romantic novel in French. They were so disappointed when I told them it would not do for my son. When we returned to the hotel, Russell confessed that he had been out to eat while we were gone. I was shocked, but he reassured me by saying, "I went to the Chinese restaurant. I thought they wouldn't notice that I was yellow."

Finally the next morning came, and we returned to the airstrip. The Jungle Aviation and Radio Service (JAARS) plane came in, and we went to Lomalinda on the first flight. When we arrived, we found that the news of the doctor's diagnosis of Russell's hepatitis had beaten us to the base. The nurses had gone into high gear in planning the isolation of the patient and his immediate family, who were all assumed to be contagious. Russell was ordered to bed rest in the cabin, and all of us except Sharon were quarantined. Sharon had been staying with another family in my absence and had not been around Russell since my departure, so she was considered uncontaminated. She was ordered to stay with her host family. The men's bathroom facilities were assigned to be used by our family only. All the other people on the base, both men and women, had to use the women's bathroom.

Just about dusk, I heard someone crying on our doorstep. It was Sharon. She said she would rather come in and die with her family and not be left in another house. Of course we took her in, and she was quarantined with us.

Hepatitis is a serious disease, and can be fatal to middle-aged and elderly people. There was no medicine known at that time, and no immunizations. A gamma globulin shot was considered to give some short-term immunity. The next day a large amount of gamma globulin was flown in, and everyone was injected.

Chad was allowed to go over to Loma II and work on our house as he would not be around other people. I believe someone brought us the children's school assignments. Russell was feeling just fine now, so it was hard to keep all the children happy in the little 12' x 20' cabin. In about a week, the nurses pronounced Russell well, and since none of the rest of us showed signs of hepatitis, we were released from the quarantine.

Soon after our release, Chad came home with the good news that our house was far enough completed, so that we could move in.

Chapter 8

Amanda Comes

Chad and I were concerned because we were spending so little time in the tribe. We reconsidered the advice given by the missionaries at Carmelo that we transfer our children to the Carmelo school. They could live in the children's home during the week, we figured, and come home to our house at Santiago's farm on the weekends. We thought we would feel more at peace knowing that our children were just four hours away down the trail, instead of some 600 miles, and several days' travel away at Lomalinda. We sent a letter to Carmelo, and talked with our director at Lomalinda. Soon it was all set. We would go to our tribal home for the summer, and when school started, Chad would just take the children down the trail to Carmelo.

This was June 1966, and after only a few weeks in our new house at Lomalinda, we packed up and took off for our tribal location by way of Bogotá. I had received a long list of all the clothes and items that the children needed to bring with them to Carmelo. It was impressive. School, as well as life at Lomalinda was informal, and the climate was hot. Carmelo was up in the cool mountains, and nights were cold. Each child needed to bring three woolen blankets in addition to a bedspread and two sets of sheets. The patchwork quilts I had made could serve as bedspreads, I decided, but I would have to purchase *nine* wool blankets in Bogotá. I remember that Sharon, as a girl, had to have a best dress, a second best dress, and five school dresses in addition to play clothes. A number of different kinds of shoes were also required. Everything had to be labeled with her name of course. The boys' requirements were similar. Instead of a best dress, they needed white shirts and ties and dress pants. All of these items had to be purchased in Bogotá. Each child packed his metal footlocker with the things that would serve for school plus all their older clothes in duffle bags to wear during the months in the tribe. I was wondering how we would manage to pay for all this. We had just barely been holding our own in keeping our account out of the red.

Upon our arrival at the Bogotá group house, a huge shock awaited us. We were met at the door by the temporary acting housemother and denied admittance. She had heard that Russell had hepatitis and would not allow us to come into the house. We had been free from quarantine in Lomalinda for several weeks, but nothing we could say would dissuade the housemother. (I believe I did get permission to enter and get some of our Bogotá clothes from the storage closet.) She gave us the names of several hotels and restaurants that she thought would be suitable.

I felt we had been dealt a huge blow below the belt. Had we been contagious, it would have been better for her, a member of our mission family, to have prepared a special room and bathroom for us and have our meals brought to us on disposable plates. I was really upset. Here we were being cast out upon the general unsuspecting public with whatever diseases we might have. However, I knew that we had been declared by the medical staff at Lomalinda to have a clean bill of health, so I wasn't too worried about the Colombian public. I was very worried about the status of our financial account. The bookkeeper gave Chad whatever money he requested, so we went to a hotel, ate in restaurants, and purchased all the items on the school list. Then we bought airplane tickets and flew to Santa Marta. There we bought about three months' worth of powdered milk, rice, canned meat, sardines, etc. and headed up the mountain road.

Leaving the children's school clothes and bedding at the children's home at Carmelo, we packed our tribal gear in duffle bags and headed up the trail. This time, instead of a strange new experience, we felt like we were coming home. Gloria was big enough now to sit in front of me on the mule. Her orthopedic brace was stored in a duffle bag for the time being. An additional person was with us on this trip. She was Lynn, a recent college graduate. She had completed a five-year course and was a registered nurse with a master's degree. She wanted to spend her summer as a missionary short-term assistant, and the director thought our tribal location would be just the place. She and Chad handled all the medical work, and she also decided that amusing Gloria would be a service she could render to me to leave me more time to deal with all my other duties. I'm sure she also lent a hand in dishwashing, etc. I appreciated her presence very much.

The story of the splinter in María Elena's hand happened on our first tribal stay and is told in *High Adventure in Colombia*. In this, our second tribal stay as a family, there is another story involving María Elena's hand. One afternoon she came to me with a very bad machete cut on her hand. Lynn was not there at the time, and I applied pressure and did all I could think of to stop the bleeding, but the bleeding did not stop. Chad tried everything he could think of too, but to no avail. We were especially concerned because María Elena was pregnant. We were very worried about all this blood loss. All of a sudden Lynn ran into the house. As soon as she realized what was happening, she raised the bleeding hand above María Elena's head and applied pressure. The bleeding slowed down, and finally stopped. This was a good lesson for Chad and me that came in handy on many future occasions. Elevate the bleeding part above the heart, if possible. Then Lynn also gently told us that we should not give bleeding patients a cup of coffee while we were trying to stop the bleeding. The caffeine made it harder for the blood to clot.

Right about the time of María Elena's hand injury, we had a visit from a group of Colombian young people who lived about two hours farther up the trail in a small community called Nueva América (New America, because just they and the Indians lived there). The mission at Carmelo maintained a small chapel there, and some of these young people were Bible school students at Carmelo and had seen us when we stayed at Carmelo on our first trip to the tribe. After all the flowery greetings and the cup of Nescafe that I gave them, they revealed the reason for their visit: One of their family members, a young man around 20, was very, very ill. In fact they despaired for his life. One of their sisters had training as a nurse, and they had brought penicillin shots from San Pedro, but nothing had helped. The young man was going downhill rapidly. Lynn and Chad talked over the symptoms and suspected typhoid fever, which does not respond to penicillin. Fortunately, they found the two drugs of choice in our medical kit. Off they went with the visitors, and the young man's life was saved. (I must mention that we always pray for the sick, and treat them medically the best we can. When they get well, we thank the Lord together with the patient and family members.)

Chad was getting ready to take the children to Carmelo to school. Lynn would go with them and continue on to Santa Marta and Bogotá. Gloria and I would stay in our house, accompanied by María Elena next door. Upon Chad's return from Carmelo, he and Santiago were planning to make a trip to the Kogi village of Don Diego to the north, Santiago's home village. About a week before this would all happen, we had a visit from Señora Raquel. She was a very well-mannered Colombian lady, the mother of the young man who had recovered from typhoid fever. She had come to pay a social call and thank us for helping her son. When she found out that Chad and the children, and Lynn as well, were all leaving, she had a fit. She insisted that I could not stay alone with the Indians.

I was rather looking forward to having them all gone. I would finally have some time to study and work on the linguistic analysis. Señora Raquel had many daughters, and she insisted that she was going to send one to accompany me. I really didn't want one, as I didn't want to have to entertain a visitor during what I considered was going to be my personal study time. She invited Chad to attend the small church in Nueva América on Sunday, and she would send a daughter home with him. When Sunday came, Lynn offered to stay with Gloria so that I could attend the service. It would be my only chance to visit the church, as Lynn would be leaving in a few days and there was no one else to take care of Gloria for a day. This whole story is told in detail in *High Adventure in Colombia.* Suffice it to say here, that when we returned home, we had Amanda with us. Far from having to wait on her as a guest, Amanda started helping with the housework as soon as she got in the door. Now, almost 50 years later, she is still our valued friend and coworker.

From the beginning of our time staying on Santiago's farm, non-Indian people visited us. We were in an area where most of the Indians had left long ago. Their land had been purchased cheaply by non-Indian Colombians. Many of these Colombian people had fled to this area to escape the ten years of political violence that had just passed. This was the case with Amanda's family. Others had sought out this remote area as a refuge from the law. The few Kogis who had held onto their lands in this area were able to somewhat coexist with the *civilizados* as they called them in Spanish. There was no love lost between the two groups. Santiago's few possessions had been stolen several times while he and María Elena were out working on their farm. The thieves hoped that by so doing they would discourage Santiago, and he would abandon his farm and move farther into the mountains. This was one of the underlying reasons that Santiago and his Kogi neighbors were willing to receive us into their area. They saw us as a protection against these aggressive newcomers.

Chad and I had to decide what our attitude would be toward the *civilizados.* Most of our Wycliffe coworkers helped only the Indians and ignored whatever white people lived in their areas. Somehow we felt that it would not be wise to follow suit. Chad had been told by the police in San Pedro that living where we were on Santiago's farm we were beyond the protection of the law. Chad didn't tell me that the police officer had predicted that within two weeks, all that we had would be stolen and Chad's wife (me) would be raped. It was just as well that I hadn't heard that prediction.

We decided that we would reach out a helping hand to Indian and non-Indian alike. Chad made many a long trip through the mud, sometimes at night, to give a penicillin shot to a sick baby or to a young mother with postpartum infection. The main trail went right past our kitchen door, and I treated every passing person to a cup of Nescafe (Colombian instant coffee) and a homemade goody or a store-bought cookie.

Soon they saw us as friendly, helpful neighbors.

Still, it was disconcerting to me that whenever I was left alone with the children, young men from the neighboring farms would come for lengthy visits. I didn't invite them into the house, but they would linger outside long after they had finished the coffee or lemonade I had given them. One in particular bothered me. He seemed a little retarded, and even with my limited Spanish, it seemed to me that he was using vulgar vocabulary. I tried to ignore these visitors and went about my work in the kitchen. I was happy now to have Amanda with me. She knew them all, where they lived and their family background and was an expert in getting rid of them.

Amanda had become a Christian through the Carmelo mission. She had been praying for the opportunity to spend more time studying the Bible. She was a sober, introverted girl, in the middle of an outgoing friendly family. They hoped that by sending her to live with us, she might become more outgoing. It worked. She told us years later that when Chad told a joke, and no one laughed (because we had all heard his jokes before), she felt that she had to laugh. Her mother had taught her that it was very impolite to let a person tell a joke and no one laugh. Little by little she thawed out and became a friendly person, and she also found a lot of time to study the Bible. She had a great love for the Kogis even before she came to live with us. She had prayed for them and wished that she could minister to them. Now she had her chance. She entered wholeheartedly into our ministry

of medical work and hospitality. (She also told us that although we considered our coffee strong, the saying among the non-Indian neighbors was: Let's go over to the *gringos'* house and drink a liter of weak coffee. They served their coffee very strong in tiny *tinto* cups, not mugs.)

Chapter 9

The Birth of Margot

When Chad returned to Santiago's farm after taking the children to Carmelo, we realized that there might be a few problems. The school consisted of two classrooms. Grades one through five were in one classroom and grades six through nine in the other. Sharon was in third grade, Chaddy in fourth, and Russell in sixth. Of the twenty children in the school, only two were girls. The only other girl was in sixth grade. That left Sharon without a girlfriend her age. The houseparents for the children's home were new this year. I don't remember if one or both of them were from England. The queen's picture was in a prominent place in the living room. Sharon had made a great faux pas by saying, "Who is that ugly lady?" I guess we had never introduced her to English royalty.

Instead of running freely over the hills of Lomalinda, their lives were now very regimented. The Canadian and English staff felt that the way to prevent trouble was to keep the children very occupied. They arose early. The boys worked in the garden for an hour before breakfast while the two girls dusted the living room and dining room. All the children had piano lessons, and their practice times were posted and enforced. I believe there were just 15 minutes of unscheduled time each day. I am not saying that this was a bad practice, but it was quite a shock for our children who were used to a more relaxed schedule. Instead of having Saturday as a free day, it was school as usual. The free day was Monday. Sunday was a very busy day with all the children in attendance at the Sunday services, the girls in their "best dresses," and the boys in their white shirts, ties, and dress pants. As I remember,

after church the girls changed to their "second best dress" and the boys to something a little less formal for the rest of the day. In the evening there was church again. All the church services were in Spanish, and our children were not very proficient yet. The school and all their daily conversation was in English (the Queen's English of course).

The first weekend Chad hiked to Carmelo on Saturday and brought the children home after school for the weekend. That made 8 hours on the trail for him on Saturday and another 8 on Monday when he took them back again. He didn't complain, but after a few weeks we were told that our children were not going to be allowed to come home on weekends, only on Christmas and Easter vacations. The reason given was that it was not fair to the other children whose parents lived far away. A secondary reason was that the children returned too tired to do well in school on Tuesday.

I could understand the second reason, but I really rebelled at the first one. Didn't they realize that this was the whole reason we brought them to Carmelo, so that we could be near them and have them home on weekends? Chad thought it better to not stir up a fuss, so we conformed to the rule. I visited Carmelo once during the first few weeks of school. The school staff was very friendly and invited us to have supper in the children's home. Sharon shared a room with the one older girl. Chaddy and Russell were each in a different room with three or four other boys their age. Everything was clean and very orderly. In the living room, below the picture of Elizabeth II, was a large circle of unmatched comfortable overstuffed chairs and sofas. The missionaries told us about a visit they had had from Santiago and his wife during the first few days of school. Santiago felt the seats of all the chairs and picked out the most comfortable for himself. Then he decided which was the second most comfortable for María Elena. The two Kogis then joined the children for their daily devotions.

A few weeks after Chad and Santiago came back from their trip to Don Diego, Amanda came down with a severe toothache. We decided she would have to go to the dentist. We took her to Carmelo and found "no room in the inn," as the guesthouse was being used by other visitors. Since the Colombian Bible Institute was not in session, we were housed in the girls' dormitory. Wouldn't you know that I picked that Sunday to come down with my second malaria attack. It was almost as bad as the first one. The good thing was that Annie Noble was there visiting, and I had her tender care plus the proper medicine from the start. The bad thing was that the bed was incredibly hard and uncomfortable. The next day was Monday, the day the Carmelo jeep made the round trip to Santa Marta and back. Someone took Amanda to the dentist. The other visiting missionaries also went in the jeep to Santa Marta, and Annie Noble made sure that I was moved to the more comfortable guesthouse.

After a few days, I started to feel better. As soon as we had arrived at Carmelo this time, Chad was told that the children's house parents thought it best that he and I did not see our children, and we were asked to not visit the school or the children's home. No one said anything to me until I was better. It seems that the other time I visited the school, Chaddy had been upset when I left. This was a terrible development. It seemed like we were more separated from our children than when they had been at Lomalinda. At least when they were at Lomalinda we could talk with them once a week on the tribal radio. That evening Chaddy was brought up to the guesthouse by his teacher. He was in tears. He knew that we were at Carmelo, and he wanted us to be invited to supper at the children's home again like we had been before. When his request was denied, he got more upset and wanted to leave Carmelo and go back to Lomalinda. In desperation, they brought him to me.

We tried to comfort him, but the school authorities weren't making any compromises, so there wasn't much we could do. Chaddy refused to be comforted. I was still very weak from the malaria, and I started to cry too. That really surprised Chaddy, as I was not in the habit of crying. He said he would go back to the school and be good, if only I wouldn't cry. (I believe Chad told him that if he would behave and get a good report from the people at Carmelo, he would return him to school at Lomalinda the next year.) Chaddy gave us each a hug and let himself be led off to the school again by his teacher. (Please let me add that both teachers were very lovely women and did a wonderful job teaching our children that year.)

Amanda had just returned from having her tooth extracted when what seemed to be a different tooth started aching. Someone was going down to Santa Marta again in the middle of the week, so we sent Amanda back to the dentist again. (It seems that the dentist had pulled the wrong tooth.) She had just returned from the second extraction when a traveler from San Javier brought us the news that María Elena, Santiago's wife, was dying in childbirth. It was already getting dark, and a terrific thunderstorm was in progress. I was much too weak to go back to our tribal location, so Chad insisted that Amanda go with him. He felt completely incapable of handling a woman dying in childbirth and thought that since Amanda was a woman herself, she would know more than he. Amanda was game to go, although she was just recovering from having her teeth pulled. She didn't know much about childbirth, but she was a calm, practical person with good sense. The Carmelo missionaries wanted to be helpful, so they insisted that she ride the mule, America. The mule was saddled and brought to the door, and off went Chad and Amanda into the storm.

No one even thought of the fact that they were leaving me alone with two-year-old Gloria, who was not yet allowed to walk because of her hip problem. I kept her in bed with me and amused her by trying to teach her to count to ten in three languages, English, Spanish, and Kogi. In between counting, I was praying for María Elena and her baby. María Elena was Santiago's third wife. His wives had had lots of babies, but only one child was living, a girl who was with her mother in Don Diego. We were all praying that this baby would make it. The counting game was just getting boring when the door swung open, and in walked Amanda. She hadn't been gone long, but she had quite a story to tell.

As I mentioned, it was lightning and thundering when Chad and Amanda left. The rain was pouring down. The road did a big switchback going uphill from Carmelo, and switching back through the town of San Pedro, straight up the mountain above the guesthouse before turning into a mule trail and heading out into the wild mountains on the way to San Javier, the town just across the steep riverbanks from Santiago's house. The trail was incredibly muddy and slippery. Haste was important, as the word was that María Elena was bleeding to death. At least Chad had an injection of vitamin K that just might help.

Amanda was riding the mule, and Chad was leading it with his hand on the bridle. The mule was terribly frightened by all the lightning and thunder and really didn't want to go. As they went through San Pedro, directly above the guesthouse, a bolt of lightning hit the metal bridle. It was probably not a direct hit, but Chad felt the electric current in his hand that was on the bridle. That did it for America. She reared up into the air, and then fell to the ground. Bystanders shouted that the mule was dead, but America struggled to her feet with Amanda still on her back. She rolled her eyes back, planted her feet, and refused to go another step. Chad had to go on alone and leave Amanda to lead America back to her stable at Carmelo.

Now there were two of us to pray for María Elena and her baby. We prayed for Chad too, as Amanda said she didn't see how he would make it to Santiago's house. During a rain like this there were always landslides on the narrow mule trail that led to San Javier. Then there was the steep descent to the river, the dangerous crossing over the log bridge, and the climb up to Santiago's house. But in those days, Chad was undaunted by difficulties. When he set his mind on a course of action, there was no stopping him.

The next day Chad returned with his own incredible story. Trees fell before him and behind him. There were several landslides behind him. Somehow he made it to Santiago's house. There he found María Isabela, a neighbor colonist woman. She had a lot of experience to her credit as she, herself, had borne 19 live babies. María Elena's baby girl was just fine, and María Elena was resting comfortably when Chad

arrived.   Santiago had overcome his natural reluctance to call for help from the *civilizados* and in his desperation sent for María Isabela. More about María Isabela and her family is told in *High Adventures in Colombia.*

Santiago was very happy with his baby girl. He promptly named her Margot after the director's wife at Carmelo. If she lived to maturity, she would bring him a son-in-law to work on his farm. María Elena already had Cecilia from an earlier marriage, so Margot would belong to Santiago. He was much happier to have a daughter to bring him a son-in-law than to have a son who would have to go and work for another family. María Elena was happy that the birth was successful and that she was still alive, but there was a big problem. In the throes of her labor, when she thought she would die, she had confessed to having committed adultery with one of the Kogi men in the area during her pregnancy. As soon as her four days of rest after bearing a child were over, Santiago marched her to San Pedro to answer to the charge before the police inspector.

We had just returned to Santiago's farm, so he left us in charge of everything, including his chickens and five-year-old Cecilia. It took them four days to get everything straightened out in San Pedro. In the meantime, I was free to use the eggs that the chickens produced. I believe both María Elena and the man involved had to pay fines to Santiago. This seemed a very strange and tragic state of affairs from our point of view, but Santiago returned content with the settlement. Fortunately there had never been a question about the parentage of the baby.

While Santiago and María Elena were gone, I enjoyed having the use of the eggs their chickens laid. Even one egg was a prize there in Kogiland. We actually had enough eggs to enjoy several meals of scrambled eggs before the owners of the chickens returned. One day soon after their arrival, I decided to bake a cake that needed one egg. I went down to the little house where the chickens had their nests and took one egg. Santiago and María Elena were out on their farm working; otherwise I would have asked them for one. They would be helping us eat the cake. Later when Santiago returned from his fields, he asked Chad why he let his wife steal. Chad was in the dark about the whole affair, but I was called to stand trial for stealing an egg. Santiago was very solemn and angry. To him it was a very serious affair. I admitted to the crime and asked forgiveness, which was rather grudgingly granted. I never went near the chicken nests again.

Another incident occurred a few months later. We began really longing for some kind of green vegetable in our diet. Evidently the porch that Chad had built along the back of the house intruded into what had been a bean field. A row of bean plants grew up close to the porch on the far side. One day I noticed that they looked just like the green beans that we are used to buying in the grocery store in the city. The green pods were tender and the beans inside were young. The Kogis never eat beans that way. They wait until the beans inside are large and mature and the pods are brown and dry, then they are harvested. These bean plants seemed to be a part of my yard and jurisdiction. One day I picked about ten or twelve green beans and broke them into pieces and cooked them for lunch. They were delicious. Once again, I was called before the judge (Santiago) to answer to the charge of stealing. Once again I apologized. Forgiveness was a little harder for Santiago to give this time. No matter that he was eating almost three meals a day with us and enjoying all kinds of delicacies from the outside world. Ownership is very important to a Kogi, and stealing is one of the worst offenses. It may even be equal to murder. For example: If you eat a stalk of plantains hanging on a tree on a deserted farm, you could be causing the death of the owner and his family. Perhaps they will come back to this farm from another area and count on eating that stalk of plantains while other crops are growing. It would be better to let the bananas rot on the tree than eat them if they don't belong to you.

After this, I was very careful to not touch anything that belonged to Santiago or María Elena without their express permission. These lessons we learned on Santiago's farm seemed hard at the time, but they were necessary to prepare us to live in a Kogi village area with a much larger population.

Chapter 10

Important Happenings

Life on Santiago's farm settled into a routine. We started taping Kogi stories for grammar analysis. Both Santiago and María Elena loved to tell stories into our small reel-to-reel tape recorder. They worked on their farm in the morning sun, and when the daily rain started they would take refuge in our house to help us with the stories. Then we would review the story by playing it back phrase by phrase and the speaker would repeat what they had said slowly so that we could write it in our notebooks. When it was all written down to the best of our ability, we would play it again piece by piece, and they would tell us what it said in Spanish. Both Santiago and María Elena were quite proficient in Spanish. Their Spanish was a simple country style that was spoken in the area using a limited vocabulary. We could soon understand them quite well.

When we got into the Spanish translation, we were surprised by the content of the stories. One day when recording, Santiago and María Elena really got wound up and vied with each other to tell short anecdotes and stories. We thought they must be Kogi jokes by the way they laughed. When we finally got them translated, we found they were tragic short stories about children and others being eaten by *tigres* (jaguars), some stolen at night right out of their houses. Others were of travelers lost in the snow in the high mountain country. Their rotting bones were found years later during an extra-warm dry season. We didn't think they were funny. Since we needed 200 pages of typed and translated text for the next linguistic workshop, we kept recording. Both María Elena and Santiago told us the stories of their lives. We were surprised to learn that they had not been together as a couple for long. Santiago had been left a widower after Alfonso's sister's death. María Elena had led a tragic life (see Minnesota Mom Volume I, *Beginnings*, Chapter 13) and drifted into this area as a single woman not long before Chad met them in October 1964.

I was shocked to learn that Santiago's first wife, Alicia, and daughter, Maldia (María) lived in Don Diego. It seemed to me that in order for Santiago to become a Christian, he and Alicia would have to reconcile. I wondered about the future for María Elena. It never even occurred to me that Alicia might have another husband and other children by now.

One day a Bible school student stopped by on his way to Nueva América. Someone had sent our accumulated mail from Lomalinda to Carmelo. He also brought us a few pounds of meat that the Carmelo missionaries guessed correctly would be a welcome addition to our diet. Amanda was a whiz at keeping meat fresh without refrigeration. She cut it in thin slices, covered the slices with salt and other spices, and divided it into daily portions that she placed in plastic bags as free of air as possible. Then she packed all the plastic bags in a milk can with a tight-fitting lid and a carrying handle. This she took to the river, tying the handle securely to a tree trunk or root, so the whole thing would not be swept away by the river. Every day, a bag could be removed for dinner. I have seen her keep meat fresh for a week that way. (I could never make it work for more than a few days.) After this, we left a standing order for meat at Carmelo whenever anyone came our way.

When we opened our mail, to our surprise we had a letter from the director dated soon after we left Lomalinda in June. In it he stated that he had been checking over the red accounts, and found that ours was one of the worst. He advised us that since we had seemed to be stockpiling supplies in June, we would not need to withdraw much in the line of funds over the next few months. I don't remember whether I wrote back telling him all that had happened to us in June, such as being banned from the group house, but the financial report from the treasurer, dated in August, showed that we were making a lot of progress in coming out of the red. I don't remember how we paid the children's expenses at Carmelo, but at any rate, we hadn't needed much money during the summer months when we were all in the tribe.

Chad and Santiago made another trip to Mamarongo. They were welcomed by Mama Nacio, who continued in good health. The young men of the area took Chad to a place where they were thinking of relocating the village. So far just two large round houses had been constructed, one for the men, the large men's council house, and a slightly smaller house for women. Chad was amazed to see that the proposed village site was at the near end of a long level gently sloping area. It actually looked like an airstrip. All that would need to be done was to cut the grass, dig out some large rocks, and cut down some trees at the end. Chad was sure a short-field airplane could land there. They all got very excited and went back to talk to Mama Nacio. He consulted with the other old men, and they ruled, no, to the airstrip idea. To their way of thinking, part of the price they had to pay for the power to bring the sun up in the morning, bring the dry season, make the seeds sprout, and other metaphysical acts was to keep away from civilized items. It might cause the end of the world if they allowed something as modern and civilized as an airplane to land in their area, they reasoned.

Santiago and the younger men were disappointed, and Chad was devastated. It seemed like such a miracle to find an ideal spot for an airstrip in the middle of such a rugged terrain. He couldn't understand why he should be denied the use of it. He had been wondering how he would ever bring all the children and me into such a remote area, and here was

 the answer ready made. Sadly, he and Santiago together with Santiago's beloved burro, made their way down the trail towards Santiago's house three days away.

The clouds were rolling in from the sea, and the place where Santiago planned to stop for the night was hours away.

As they passed a small round Kogi house, Chad noticed an elderly woman sitting on a rock. She was doubled over as if in pain. Chad sensed the inward voice of the Lord saying, "Do all you can for her."   He stepped off the trail to go over to see what the problem was.   This annoyed Santiago, who firmly told him that they had no time to stop. They had to keep going in order to get to their destination before the rain hit.

Chad continued over to the old woman.   He found that she had a bad infection in one side of her head.   She was blind in that eye and deaf in that ear.   She also had very bad stomach pains.   She was just sitting on that rock waiting to die.

Santiago wanted to keep going, but Chad pulled the slipknot on the rope that was holding the duffle bags onto the burro.   The duffle bags fell to the ground, and that effectively made forward progress impossible.   Chad opened the first duffle bag, and right on top he found some ear drops, some eye drops, pain pills, and a general antibiotic.   He gave all these medicines to the old woman with instructions to her and her family as to their use.   He prayed for her, and then they tied the duffle bags on the burro and were on their way.

When he got back to our little house on Santiago's farm, he was still very depressed.   He just couldn't understand why there should be such an ideal place for an airstrip and the use of it be denied him.   A week went by.   One afternoon three Kogi men arrived at Santiago's farm.   They were from Mamarongo, and they had been traveling as fast as they could go.   They were very excited.

"Do you remember that little old woman that you helped on your way out of Mamarongo?" one of the men asked Chad through Santiago.   "Well, that was my mother.   She is just fine now.   She can see and hear and has no pain.   She is the owner of that piece of land where you want to build an airstrip.   She says you can come and build an airstrip there anytime you want to.   So do all the rest of us.   We want you to come and show us how to do it."

In October the so-called walking tip broke off of Gloria's brace.   As I mentioned before, this brace was an ingenious invention to prevent Gloria from placing weight on her left hip joint.   She was never able to learn to walk with it, but it did keep her from standing up and injuring her bad hip. She had already outgrown the shoes that went with the brace, one normal, and one built up to match the elevation of the other foot. I solved that problem by cutting out the toes of the shoes to give her feet more room, but now she had broken off the tip of the brace, so the whole thing was worthless. We didn't have the time nor money to go back to Bogotá, so the missionaries at Carmelo referred us to an orthopedic specialist in Barranquilla, one of the large cities of Colombia, which was just some two hours to the west of Santa Marta. They also made arrangements for us to stay in the group house of one of their sister missions in Barranquilla.

After looking at the X-rays, the new orthopedic specialist expressed doubt that Gloria had ever had a congenital hip dislocation. "They never turn out this good," he mumbled. However, he said that the neck of the left femur had been injured, probably while she was in traction, and because of this, her left leg was always going to be shorter than her right one. His opinion was that there was no reason to keep her from walking. "Just let her walk and we will see how much disability she will have," he said. When I demurred, he was insistent.

"I want to see her walk out of my office," he stated firmly.

Up until this time, whenever Gloria tried to put weight on her left leg, I would sit her down firmly saying, "The doctor says you can't stand up."

Now, as we stood her on the doctor's examining table, she said, "Can I stand up?"

"Yes," I said, "The doctor wants to see you walk."

Remember, she was now 26 months old, and she had never walked before. I stood her on the floor, and she took off running. As soon as the doctor dismissed us, she ran out of his office and down the sidewalk with Chad and me right behind her. I believe we ran for blocks, laughing all the way. Chad, who was taller than most Colombians, cracked his head on an overhanging tree branch, but not even that slowed us down much.

Back at Carmelo, everyone rejoiced with us, and of course we had to see the children and show them Gloria walking. Everyone seemed to forget about keeping the children and us apart. I wrote letters home to our parents and friends. When Gloria was very small in Lomalinda, she used to sit in her chair and say, "Deedle, deedle, deedle." In fact sometimes the older children called her Deedle as a nickname.   Gloria realized that I was writing a letter to send to the grandparents. "Did you tell them about Walky Deedle?" she asked me.

One day soon after our return from Barranquilla, I asked Chad when we were going to take our vacation. As members of Wycliffe, we were allowed one month of vacation a year. It was felt that the intensity of our life in the tribe and also at Lomalinda when we were in a workshop or language analysis situation demanded that we take some time off for rest and recuperation. This vacation could be taken all at once, or split up in shorter periods of time scattered throughout the year. Some families went on a trip, others to the beach.   Some just relaxed at Lomalinda.   Others with good support money sometimes went back to the States for a short visit with their families and supporters. As far as I knew, Chad and I had never taken any formal vacation time. I tried to make every minute of my time count, jungle-camp style. Even when we went to Barranquilla, I took along correspondence and paperwork to be done in odd minutes. I was surprised by Chad's answer to my above question.

"You just had your vacation in Barranquilla," he told me.

I asked him to please let me know in advance the next time we were going to take vacation time. Chad learned from traveling with Uncle Cam Townsend to always have a swimsuit in his suitcase. If a flight was delayed or some other circumstance caused an unplanned delay, a mini-vacation could be worked in on the spot. Once, this happened at the Santa Marta airport. A flight was delayed, so Uncle Cam went swimming in the ocean. (Chad could only watch, as he hadn't learned to carry his swimsuit with him yet.) Uncle Cam had a wonderful swim all by himself on a deserted beach. Later, the locals informed him that the waters near the airport were shark-infested.

We returned to our tribal home. True to his word, Santiago came to our kitchen mid-morning to eat any leftovers and keep us from feeding his dog. As he felt more at home with us, he would reveal more and more details of the Kogi life and culture, as well as his personal history. One day as he relaxed in one of our green and white plastic web folding chairs, he mentioned, "The outside people call us *Kogis*, but we call ourselves *Kagaba*, the real people. We call our language *Kaugian.*" The word *Kagaba* had a familiar sound to me; surely I had heard it before. A while later it dawned on me: *Kagaba* was the first and most oft repeated word in my prayer language. The Holy Spirit had been praying for this tribe through my lips, even before I had ever heard of them.

Chapter 11

A Door is Closed

As November drew to a close, a message from the director reminded us that our presence was required in Lomalinda for a week in mid-December to attend the annual conference. Officers would be elected, business matters would be discussed and put to a vote, and a pastor or evangelist would be coming from the United States to bring us morning and evening Bible-teaching messages. This was always a very special time of both physical and spiritual refreshment for all of us missionaries. Everyone had to leave his or her tribal locations and gather at Lomalinda. This usually worked out well for the translators. They could spend Christmas and New Year's with their children before returning to their tribes again in January.

This year we had complicated the situation by moving our children to Carmelo; however, there was time for us to attend the conference in Lomalinda and still return to spend the holidays with the children in our tribal location. The missionaries at Carmelo couldn't believe we were going all the way back to the eastern Llanos again, but we assured them that we would be back in time to pick up our children when they were dismissed for Christmas vacation.

Just before we left our tribal location, we had received a note delivered by one of the passing Bible institute students.

Our good friends in Santa Marta had been transferred to another location, and a different missionary couple was stationed in Santa Marta. The note was from them. They were having a cursillo (an intensive time of Bible teaching) the weekend that we were planning to be in Santa Marta on our way back to Lomalinda. The note was to inform us that they would be very busy that weekend, and it would not be convenient for them to have us show up at the mission house or church at all. This was kind of like a bucket of cold water dumped on our heads. We had left a small suitcase at the mission house containing our Bogotá clothes. We needed to get that suitcase before leaving for Bogotá. However, we could understand that the missionaries were going to be very busy that weekend, and we didn't want to add stress to the situation.

Upon our arrival at Carmelo, we were asked to drive the mission jeep down to Santa Marta and leave it at the mission house that was connected to the church. The director had traveled to Santa Marta with someone else, and now he needed the jeep to get back up the mountain to Carmelo. Of course we were glad to comply with the request. It would solve our transportation problem, and since we had to go to the mission house to leave the jeep, we could pick up our suitcase at the same time.

We were very tired after traveling the treacherous mountain road down to the low country. Just before arriving at Santa Marta, there was a beautiful sandy beach called El Rodadero. This was the tourist area of Colombia. As we drove by in the jeep, we noticed that a beautiful new hotel had been built by the beach. It was probably a two- or three-star operation, but to me after living for months on Santiago's farm, it looked like an example of absolutely sinful luxury.

Chad persuaded me that we should stop for a rest. He overcame my protests and got me into the air-conditioned restaurant for a ham and cheese sandwich and a Coca Cola with ice. It was very nice to relax in this lovely cool place and enjoy the ocean view. I hadn't realized before how tired I was. Chad went to ask about the hotel rates. Since we couldn't stay with the missionaries, we might just as well have a night in this beautiful place, he was thinking. I don't remember how much it was going to cost, but I absolutely nixed that idea. Finally he came back with the news that we could rest for one hour in one of the lovely rooms for 100 pesos, the equivalent of about $10.00 in those days.

I absolutely had a fit. I could not in any way condone such a waste of money, I told him. I got him back into the jeep, and I told him I would find us an economical place to spend the night. I did. It was in the center of Santa Marta in a very cheap hotel. The room only cost 35 pesos, something around $3.50 USD. It was an inside room with no windows, but there was an oscillating fan, I was told. Remember that this was in the very hot city of Santa Marta. Chad left Gloria and me at the hotel and continued on to the mission house where he left the jeep and picked up our suitcase. The beds were hard, and the pillows were what Chad refers to as "dogs." We had to use a communal bathroom out in the hall, but I think we managed to get some sleep.

It was hard to tell when morning arrived as the windowless room was in perpetual darkness. When I awakened, I heard water running, and I assumed that one of the guests was taking a shower in the bathroom next to our room. I dozed off again while waiting for the person to finish his shower. I woke up again, but the water was still running. I finally despaired that the person would ever get done with his shower, so I turned on the light. It was later than I thought. I cautiously opened the door, and to our great surprise, it was raining outside. The water we heard was not from the shower, but the rain on the tin roof. We were both happy to find the bathroom unoccupied, and we got ourselves dressed and got out of that hotel as quickly as we could, even though we had to wait at the airport for several hours for our flight to Bogotá. That night has gone down in Stendal family lore as a horrible example of Mom's economizing.

It was very strange to be back at Lomalinda and living in our new house with only Gloria. Other missionaries had rented our house in our absence while waiting for their house to be built. A chubasco had lifted off part of our living room roof, but someone had replaced it and charged the new sheets of roofing to our account. The furniture that had crowded our little cabin looked sparse in a three-bedroom house. I set up three of the green and white folding chairs in a row to take the place of a sofa. (We had a set of four. One was in the tribe, and three were at Lomalinda.) Everyone was happy to see Gloria walking. The conference week passed quickly, and after buying a few presents in Bogotá, we were soon on our way back to Carmelo again.

Lots of cars had made the tortuous trip up the steep mountain road to pick up their children for the holidays. Our kids were happy to accompany us back to our little house on Santiago's farm. We had great plans for the vacation time. First of all, Luis and his family were raising a turkey for our Christmas dinner. Amanda was back and would help me figure out how to cook it on our Coleman stove. We invited them over to help us eat their turkey. Of course Santiago, María Elena, Alfonso, and Cecilia were there too, as well as the baby, Margot. I produced a wrapped gift for each one present. Luis's wife, Josefina, carefully folded each precious sheet of gift wrap to save for another use. I believe at this time they had two boys and two girls, just as we did. The turkey was definitely not a "Butterball." It was quite tough, and the breast meat was meager, but between Amanda and me we managed to turn it out tasty and chewable.

Soon after Luis and his family left for their home, the clouds unleashed the last rainfall of the season. We now would be in *verano* (summer), actually the dry season. This season lasts roughly three months, Christmas to Easter. The other season is *invierno* (winter) or the nine-month rainy season. The temperature does not vary a great deal between these two seasons, but the rainfall, which turns into snow in the high altitudes, does cool things down. On the western slopes of the Sierra Nevada de Santa Marta, the rainy season is very wet. Torrents of rain fall just after noon about every third day. On the other days a lot of water comes down, but the deluge is more moderate. During the dry season, that third-day torrent becomes a mild shower. The other days are dry. Verano is travel time in the Sierra. The muddy trails become much dryer. Volunteer work crews in both Indian and non-Indian communities attempt to level out the deep ruts made in the rainy season by the pack mules and improve the trails. Chad was planning to use this time to broaden his knowledge of the different Kogi communities. He was also planning to take Russell and Chaddy with him.

Santiago was eager to take Chad to visit Don Diego, his home village. He was sure that the influence of his friend, Mama Simon, would lead to an invitation for us to live in Don Diego. He had sent a message asking Mama Simon to send a pack buey (ox) to carry the sleeping bags and medicines. He really didn't want to risk his "magic ox" on such a trip.

As soon as Christmas was over, Chad wanted to get started. Every day they waited for Mama Simon's ox to show up, another day of the boys' vacation was gone. Finally Chad put some pressure on Santiago to come up with an alternate plan for transportation. One of the other Kogi neighbors was named Ramon. His wife Manuela owned a large black ox. On one of his early trips alone to Santiago's farm, Chad had treated Manuela for a snake bite. She had fully recovered, and her gratefulness led her to lend Chad her ox. The story of this trip is told in *High Adventure in Colombia*. Chad arrived in Don Diego right while the unfriendly Mamas were brewing up a witchcraft curse to kill him in the Páramo, high mountain country. He ended up falling in the river and being swept downstream just before arriving at Mama Simon's house. Santiago went into high gear and caught up with him and pulled him out of the ice-cold water. Mama Simon was quite confused because he knew of the curse that his colleagues were conjuring up, but here was their supposed victim at his door safe and sound although a little wet. He finally let Chad and Santiago in to dry themselves at his fire. His hospitality was rewarded by the healing of his son from some terrible disease, possibly smallpox.

In spite of Mama Simon's friendship, the enemies prevailed, and the door was tightly shut as far as the invitation to live in Don Diego was concerned. Santiago was terribly disappointed, and Chad was too of course, but the Lord had other plans.

After the children went back to Carmelo to school, Chad and Santiago returned to Mamarongo to help the young men there prepare the airstrip. To his surprise he found that they had very few metal tools. For example, there were only two worn-out axes in the entire valley. To dig out the rocks, they used *cavadores,* primitive hoes. Because of the scarcity of tools, or perhaps it was Kogi culture, only a few men worked at a time, and the others stood around ruminating a wad of coca leaves and fiddling with their *poporos,* as we learned their gourds and sticks were called in Spanish. After a while the workers laid down their tools and took out their poporos, and others picked up the tools and started working. Some of the rocks were so large that it took the strength of almost all present to remove them from the holes where they had been embedded for centuries after the Kogi men loosened the earth around them and pried them loose with the cavadores.

We learned that most of the Kogis did not have Spanish names. Each one had a secret Kogi name that was said in his presence only when he was a child. When he or she knew what his name was, it was never used in his hearing again. At least that is what we were told. Santiago would sometimes tell us the Kogi name of someone, but Alfonso never would. He was very much afraid that we would slip and say the name in front of the individual or a near relative. Then he would be in trouble. The names I am using in this story, such as Santiago, María Elena, Alfonso, Wenceslau, etc. were Spanish names that had stuck. These individuals with Spanish names were those who sallied out into the Spanish-speaking world on occasion, and the first thing they were asked was, what is your name? Some of the people who came to visit us made up a name on the spot, or Santiago named them as he introduced them to us. Many of these names stuck. The problem was that sometimes a whole family of sisters gave us the same name, such as Margarita. Or all the sons of a family used their father's name, such as Jose Antonio. This made it hard for us to distinguish individuals, and it made it next to impossible to keep medical records. We learned to refer to people by their kinship ties to someone with a well-established name.

One day a new woman showed up in Santiago's house. She was introduced to us as 'Sabel (Isabel), from Don Diego. With her arrival we learned a new Spanish word, *celos* (jealousy). María Elena went around with a grumpy attitude and frowning face. When we asked what the problem was, Santiago said, "Celos."

I believe it was 'Sabel who started the custom of using our Missionary Equipment Service's hand-powered washing machine to "wash" her clothes. It stood in our backyard under the clotheslines. Before Amanda came to live with us, Alfonso had to carry water to fill the machine. A wedge-shaped plunger agitated the water as one moved the handle from side to side. On one end was a hand-powered wringer. I had a large plastic tub filled with rinse water to catch the clothes as they came through the wringer from the washer and the soapy water. Then after rinsing, the clothes were put back through the wringer by reversing the motion, and the clean rinse water was wrung from the clothes. Then they were hung on the clotheslines to dry.

Since Amanda's arrival, she took the dirty clothes to the river and washed them there. They turned out cleaner, and it saved all the carrying of water. María Elena must have explained some of this to 'Sabel. She started putting her dirty clothes through the wringer dry. She would put them through one way, and then put them through the reverse direction, and hang them on the line. This was truly a "dry-cleaning" method, as the clothes never got wet. I tried to explain that this was not the way to do it, but she wasn't convinced. Soon other visitors were doing the same thing. It was hard to get the heavy clothes through the wringer without the weight of the water in the tank to hold it steady. They were yanking and jerking the wringer and machine all around in the effort to get their heavy garments through the wringer. I was afraid the whole thing would soon be broken. I tried to prevent them from doing this, but even men were sneaking out into the backyard and "washing" their clothes while I was busy cooking or tending the sick in the house. Finally Chad took the wringer off the machine and put it up under the eaves. They probably thought this was very selfish of us to deny them this easy way of doing their laundry.

'Sabel did not stay at Santiago's house for very long. We were told that she was in transit, and she must have been, as one morning she was gone. María Elena looked noticeably happier after 'Sabel's departure.

Chapter 12

Tribal Life Continues

After the children returned to school after Christmas vacation, Chad and I devoted ourselves to the task of language analysis, especially the Kogi alphabet and the gathering of the 200 pages of text. I was working with Alfonso every day, trying to teach him to read, but it just wasn't clicking. I had made a trial reading book, but Alfonso just didn't get it. He was doing quite well in arithmetic though, and his skill in copying words was improving.

Visitors, both Indian and non-Indian, continued to frequent our house. The benches alongside the kitchen walls were usually occupied. Chad built a large lean-to or porch on the back side of the house. This became our study area. Amanda was a great help as she cooked, handled the visitors, and kept our dirt floors swept and well packed with damp earth. I disliked the days when she carried all our dirty clothes to the river and spent the day washing them and drying them by laying them on grassy areas or hanging them from tree branches, leaving me to handle all the household duties and visitors alone.

One day I took Gloria and went to the river to wash, leaving Amanda to handle the kitchen and the visitors. The river was swift and cold. Gloria played happily on the riverbank until she slipped on the wet grass and fell into the raging river. I thanked God that she was upstream, and the current carried her close enough to me that I could grab the skirt of her pink dress as she was swept past me down the swift cold river. It was a very close call. After that, Gloria and I stayed at the house and let Amanda do the washing.

Amanda and I continued to feed all the people who were at our house at mealtime. The Kogis were bringing us large bundles of the bananas, plantains, yuca, and other root vegetables that they grew on their little farms, so food Kogi style was not a problem. Our water still had to be carried all the way from the river, and the wastewater had to be carried out to be thrown over the side of the mountain. I am kind of clumsy, and when a lot of people were sitting on the benches, I was afraid I might step on their bare feet with my heavy rubber boots or tennis shoes. I asked Santiago to teach me a phrase in Kogi, something like "excuse me" that I could say when I was going to carry a pan of wastewater past the people sitting on the benches. It worked wonderfully well. As soon as I said it, all the people tucked their feet as far under the bench as they could. Later I found out that it meant, "I am going to step on your feet now." Evidently there was no Kogi equivalent of "excuse me."

In the evening after the dishes had been washed, Amanda and I read the Bible by the light of the Coleman lantern. Sometimes Santiago, María Elena, or Alfonso joined us as well. I had a Spanish-English Bible, and Amanda had her Spanish Bible. We started in Mark. Amanda read slowly in Spanish. I followed along in my bilingual Bible. The others listened. This was a helpful time for all of us. It furthered my Spanish language learning immensely. After the Bible reading, we prayed. I became a little annoyed, as Amanda's prayers were so lengthy. She prayed in great depth for each request, and I felt she didn't leave me anything to pray for. It was just as well though, as I wasn't very fluent yet in praying in Spanish. The custom is to use a different grammatical form when speaking to the Deity. It is something like thee and thou in English. Not only the pronoun but also the verb endings change. It took me a while to learn to do it right. (In classical Spanish, this familiar form would also be used to speak to children or family members. In Colombia this form was only used by the upper classes in Bogotá and in prayer.)

On Sunday mornings, Amanda and I conducted a Sunday school for whatever children happened to be around. Gloria and Cecilia were regulars. Luis and Josefina's four older children usually came over. María Elena often joined us with baby Margot. Amanda had a good singing voice and knew dozens of children's choruses. Between us we told Bible stories, sometimes with pictures or flannelgraph figures. This was usually done in Spanish, but sometimes we tried to figure out how to say part of the story in Kogi. Santiago or María Elena would explain things to the others in their own language. (An interesting story of one Sunday morning is told in *High Adventures in Colombia*.)

Chad was still anxious to travel to other parts of the Kogi tribe. He wanted to check out all the different areas to make sure there was not a dialect difference. It would be sad to learn and translate the New Testament into a sub-dialect that would not serve for the entire tribe. He wanted to visit the area on the eastern side of the mountains, but Santiago told him that it would be very unlikely that he would be welcomed over there. Our other Kogi neighbors realized that we had tape-recorded Santiago and María Elena's voices. They too wanted to record tapes for us. Chad got the idea of recording messages from the Kogis who lived near Santiago, who had become our friends. These he would be able to play for the Kogis on the eastern side of the mountains. It would be like letters of recommendation.

Then we got another bright idea. María Elena was from that side of the mountains. She hadn't seen her mother and father for many years. I thought of my parents so far away in Minneapolis and how happy they would be if I showed up for a visit. (We had taped, but not yet translated her life story; see Minnesota Mom, Volume I, *Beginnings*, Chapter 13.) Wouldn't it be nice for Santiago and María Elena to accompany Chad as guides and visit María Elena's parents? Wrong! It was not a good idea!

We were quite ignorant of many Kogi customs at that time. We knew about the custom of "bride service," the husband working for his father and mother-in-law like Jacob did for Laban in the Old Testament, but we didn't realize all the ramifications involved. Santiago had never worked for María Elena's parents. They had just found each other as two single adults after Santiago's wife had drowned, and María Elena's husband had kicked her out and gotten another wife. Santiago's farm was on the very western outskirts of the Kogi area. María Elena had dropped out of view as far as her parents were concerned. By taking her back to visit her parents, we opened a Pandora's Box of events that would not have a happy ending.

While Chad and the Kogis were gone, Amanda, Gloria and I continued our accustomed life in the little house on the ridge. One day Amanda went for a visit to her home in Nuevo America for a few days. One of the missionaries at Carmelo had given us a large female calico cat named Pretty. Since Gloria and I were alone in the house, we slept together in the big bed made by zipping Chad's and my sleeping bags together. Early in the morning, Gloria woke up shouting, "Kitties! Kitties!" A black one had just been born, and a white one was already wiggling around in the sleeping bag between Gloria and me.

We had prepared a cardboard box with clean rags for the birthing occasion, but Pretty had found a better place. We carefully removed the little family to the cardboard box, and soon a striped kitten made its appearance, followed by Spotty. The white one was the biggest, and Spotty was the runt. Gloria has always had a special place in her heart for kittens. She spent most of her time from then on watching and playing with the kittens.

As soon as they returned from the other side of the mountains, Santiago told me that the trip had been a mistake. The old father-in-law had lost an arm years before in a trapiche accident. He needed to keep a son-in-law working for him all the time. He accomplished this by breaking up his daughters' marriages, so that he could get them back again as single women and get another man to come to work for them. Santiago told me how the old man tried to get him to stay and work for a different daughter named Tomasa who was single at the time. Somehow he didn't even give Santiago the option of working for María Elena. He would get another man to work for her. Santiago was irate and also I detected, scared. He didn't want to lose María Elena, and he certainly didn't want to be separated from Margot who belonged to him and gave him hopes of having a son-in-law slave himself some day in the future. Margot was still too young to leave María Elena. He knew his culture, and he knew that not even his strong will and dictatorial ways could hold his family intact. He said that only the forcefulness of Chad had gotten María Elena away from her family again, and it was not over.

From Chad's viewpoint, the trip was a success. He was convinced that the Kogis on the eastern side of the mountains spoke basically the same dialect as Santiago and Alfonso.

Chapter 13

Growth

Sometime in the spring of 1967, Chad and I together with Alfonso and Gloria took off for the literacy workshop at Lomalinda. Once again we left Russell, Chaddy, and Sharon at school in Carmelo. More families had arrived at Lomalinda. The translation center was growing. A new school building was up over beyond Loma 1. A small store, *comisariato* we called it, and a post office were new additions to Loma 1. A translation center was also going up right across from our old cabin. The rumor was that it would be air-conditioned. Our friends, Paul and Edna Hedland, translators for the Tunebo tribe, built their house right on the same hilltop that we had selected on Loma 2. Now we had neighbors. Gloria was still not able to walk long distances, and at two-and-a-half, she was heavy to carry. Chad bought a red wagon, so we could pull her over to Loma 1.

There had been more conversions among the Colombian neighbors and the Indians who were at Lomalinda for the workshop. Someone started a weekly Bible study, and Alfonso attended. The first time he went, Chad walked with him over to the Bible study. It was just at dusk, after dinner. Since we were in classes all day, I chose that time to clean the refrigerator. I ended up with a plate piled high of leftovers that had been left in the refrigerator too long. Stale mashed potatoes were perhaps the most identifiable substance. The moon was out and was casting shadows in the backyard. I was heading for our "posthole" to dispose of the heaped-up plate of garbage. I identified a round shadow that looked like the hole. While focusing on the round shadow in the distance, to my great surprise, I stepped completely unaware smack in the middle of the real posthole. My right leg was in the hole; the plate of garbage went up in the air and came down right on top of my head. My left leg with my bad knee doubled under me, but with the horror of having my other leg deep in the garbage hole, I gave a mighty push with my left foot and my right leg came out of the hole. This was all accomplished in one quick motion, faster than it takes to tell. I felt excruciating pain in my left foot, but at least I was out of the garbage hole.

Chad had bought a reclining chair in Bogotá against my protestations that we couldn't afford it. It was a chair with a collapsible chrome base that could go into a feet-up reclining position. It was covered with a red canvas material. I hobbled to the chair and collapsed. This was the first time I had ever relaxed in this chair. Chad came home and couldn't believe what he saw. He had left me washing dishes in the kitchen and returned ten minutes later to find me in the reclining chair covered with mashed potatoes and with a severe foot injury. There was no X-ray machine at Lomalinda nor in the nearby town of Puerto Lleras. I would have had to fly to Bogotá to get my foot X-rayed. The nurses and I decided that an elastic bandage and rest would do the job. We had just purchased an office chair on wheels, so I put my left knee on the chair and scooted around the house, pushing with my right leg. That gave me mobility to get around the house, and hopefully my left foot got a rest for a few days.

It seemed that everyone in Lomalinda wanted to come over to hear firsthand about my accident. I got to sit in the recliner and entertain visitors for a few days. (Maybe that was my vacation.) I probably should have gone to Bogotá as X-rays many years later show a gap in the outside bone in my left foot. However, after a few days the swelling went down, and the pain went away, and I resumed my normal activities.

Towards the end of the literacy workshop, the famed consultant Sarah Gudchinsky came for lectures. She also granted private interviews with some of us translators. She questioned me thoroughly about the Kogi tribe, their customs and diet. Then she remarked, "I think your people have a severe protein deficiency. You will have to work on upgrading the diet of the children. Then the next generation of children will be able to learn to read."

This was not what I wanted to hear. I had been trained as a teacher, and literacy was my "thing." I was not happy about having to wait for the next generation. I did not take her advice too seriously, but I did take every opportunity to upgrade the Kogi diet, especially for the children.

The time of the workshop passed rapidly, and we were soon on our way back to Carmelo again.

Chapter 14

Snakes, Bandits, & Plagues

Back at Carmelo, we received unsettling news. María Elena's father and mother (the same couple as told about in Minnesota Mom 1, *Beginnings*, Chapter 13) had come from the other side of the mountains. In fact they were at Santiago's house right now. They were insisting on taking little Cecilia home with them as a substitute for Santiago's bride service. She was now five, and they figured it wouldn't be too long before they could get a husband for her. That night we prayed earnestly about the situation, and in the morning early, Chad hit the trail for Santiago's house to try to prevent them from taking Cecilia. By now she was like a member of our own family.

Chad returned the next day. The in-laws had left without taking Cecilia. She cut her foot very deeply on a rock. The grandparents correctly assumed that she would not be able to walk so far with this foot injury. They had left, but they would return, they said. Chad had offered them money to relinquish their claims to Cecilia, but they had turned it down.

About this time we became acquainted with several Peace Corps workers. This was a program for American young people to serve in third-world countries, helping in community development and in other key areas, including health and nutrition. Some of these workers stopped to visit us when they were in our area. One of these workers brought us our first copy of *The Cross and the Switchblade*. Chad and I were quite impacted by this book. I remembered reading about Dave Wilkerson in *Time* magazine before we came to Colombia. This had been the courtroom incident in New York where he showed up waving his Bible. *Time* had tried to make him look like a fool, but I respected him and identified with his testimony of turning off the television set and spending the time more profitably. I too had been led to do the same thing right about the same time.

In *The Cross and the Switchblade* we learned for the first time about the drug use and addiction in the big cities of the United States. To our knowledge, that had not been a big problem before we came to Colombia. Now, we found ourselves living in the middle of the "cocaine eaters." All the adult Kogi men used coca, the basic ingredient of cocaine, all the time. They rolled a wad of specially treated leaves around inside their mouths while activating the cocaine by powdered lime. The lime was carried in a special gourd. A long stick was used to extract the powder. First they moistened the end of the stick with saliva and then they introduced it into the hole in the top of the gourd. Lime powder, the caustic kind, stuck to the stick, which they then put into their mouth. While they were rolling the leaves and lime around in their mouth, they made fiddling motions with the stick and the gourd, building up a ridge of saliva and lime powder around the opening. This action was incessant whenever their hands were not otherwise occupied. When they needed to talk or drink coffee, etc., the wad of leaves was spat on the floor or ground, yes, even our floor. That was why I was glad the floor was of dirt. I could sweep loose dirt onto it and then sweep the whole mess out the door and over the side of the mountain. The same was true of vomit, baby feces, etc.

After reading *The Cross and the Switchblade*, Chad and I prayed, earnestly asking the Lord that our children be spared and protected from the use of addictive drugs in any form. Now, about 50 years later, I can say that the Lord has answered our prayer.

By this time we had the little phonograph records and hand-powered phonographs to play the Gospel Recordings messages and could distribute them to the Kogis. Chad took a phonograph and a set of records to Wenceslau's house and played them for the family. When he returned, he told me that the baby was crying a lot. His stomach was hard, and he seemed to be constipated. We decided that I should go to see about the baby. I took off with a big walking stick and the dog for company.

The mountain trail was littered with leaves that had fallen. In the tropics there is no special time when leaves fall like in the temperate zones. Different trees shed their leaves at different times, but mostly in the dry season. My progress was fairly slow as I never was very good on uphill trails. Downhill was difficult for me too because of the strain it put on my bad knee. In this country, if you are not going uphill, you are probably going downhill. The dog was running back and forth finding interesting scents along the way. A small green wiggling worm, just ahead of me and to the left of the trail, caught her attention. She seemed to be a little bit frightened by it and was cautiously investigating while barking loudly. I was tempted to swat at the worm with my walking stick as I passed by. The visible part was obviously the tail, but it occurred to me that it would be good to see what the head looked like before I gave it a swat. My eyes followed the creature as it disappeared under the dry leaves on the trail. Then I noticed that it came out from the leaves on the right side of the trail and closer to me. It was quite a bit bigger around. After following a few loops with my eyes, I came to the head. It was a huge snake, and the head was right by my right ankle, ready to strike. I went straight up in the air in fright, and came down swinging my stick, swatting not the tail, but the head of the big snake. I didn't quit swatting until the snake was quite dead. I tossed the dead body over the mountainside with my stick.

I was still shaken when I arrived at Wenceslau's house. After treating the baby successfully, I told the Indians about the snake. From my description, they decided it was not poisonous, but I still was glad it was dead.

One time when we arrived at our tribal location on Santiago's farm, we found the Kogis all very upset. Santiago explained that there was a huge problem among the Kogis on the other side of the mountains. A band of bandits, led by a woman, was terrorizing them. The bandits sneaked into the Kogi houses while they slept and stole their belongings. The bandits were even threatening the lives of the Kogis. (This was before the days of guerrillas or paramilitaries in this area.) The Kogis were afraid that these bandits and their woman leader would slit their throats or cut off their heads as they slept. Chad, as the defender of the Kogi tribe, thought to put a stop to this. Taking along Santiago and Alfonso, they went to the police station in Santa Marta. The police assigned a corporal, Cabu Ortega, to take care of this problem. I think in the long run it was proven that this group of bandits, and especially their leader, did not exist. It was an invention of the Kogi mind made paranoid by constant coca use, and the story passed from person to person, village by village until most Kogis believed it to be true. When the story arrived to where Santiago lived on his isolated farm on the western slopes of the mountains, it had become a very serious problem. Cabu Ortega, Chad and the Kogis made a number of trips up into the mountains investigating these stories. It gave Chad more exposure to different areas of the tribe and put him in the best possible light as the champion of the Kogi people.

Before this rumor was put to rest, Chad and the Kogis made a lot of trips to the Santa Marta police station, and Chad became good friends with the officials there, especially when he identified himself as a former captain in the U.S. military. He was allowed to stay at the officers' quarters, and to buy at the police commissary. The police are a national organization in Colombia, not local like in the United States. They are something like the "Mounties" of Canada. C.A.R.E. had started a program in Colombia, perhaps connected with the Peace Corps. They set up hot lunch programs for school children in underprivileged neighborhoods. They sent large sacks of nutritious high-protein food for poor families, and also large bags of powdered milk. The police offered to give Chad some of this food for the Kogis. I told Chad that we particularly needed powdered milk as our supply was running low.

One time when Chad, Santiago, and Alfonso were in Santa Marta, the word came over our tribal radio that Pastor Brokke of our home church in Minneapolis and his wife were going to be in Bogotá and wanted to see Chad and me. Somehow I was able to get word to Chad through our Wycliffe office in Bogotá. He and the Kogis with him decided to travel to Bogotá on the train. I was completely tied up in the tribe with kittens and sick babies. Some kind of a very bad respiratory illness was going around.

There was a special fast train that arrived in Bogotá in 24 hours after leaving Santa Marta. Chad and the Kogis arrived without incident and had a wonderful visit with the Brokkes. The visitors said that the high point of their trip was meeting Santiago and Alfonso.

Meanwhile, back in the tribe, Amanda and I were deluged with sick people. Two, a teenager and a man, seemed to have appendicitis. We prayed for them and sent them both down the trail to the doctor in Santa Marta with a borrowed horse so they could take turns riding. Halfway down to Santa Marta, they both got well. They turned around and came back, returning the horse to its owner. Luis and Josafina's newborn baby was sick. Kogis were straggling in from other villages, dirty, unkempt, and in rags. Malnourishment was evident in their yellow skin, thin, scanty hair, and skinny bodies. We had come to realize that Santiago was our self-appointed caretaker. The Kogis had to go to his house first and show the gift they were bringing us (foodstuffs from their farms). If Santiago considered it good enough, he brought them up to our house and translated for us. That way we never got to try out our language skills with monolingual Kogis. Now that he was in Bogotá, everyone was free to come without Santiago's interference. It was rather overwhelming.

At last I radioed a message to Lomalinda asking them to tell Chad to come back. By now María Elena and her baby, Margot, were sick as well as Gloria. Lomalinda sent the message on to Chad in Bogotá. When Chad relayed the news to Santiago, his reaction was unexpected. "If my burro dies, it is your fault, and you will have to buy me another one."

"Your burro isn't even sick," responded Chad in surprise.

"No, but if my wife is sick, she can't take care of my burro, and if it dies, it is your fault," insisted Santiago.

In a few days, Chad, Santiago, and Alfonso were home. As they swaggered up the trail in their clean white clothes, Alfonso and Santiago looked bigger, healthier, and much more capable than the sick Kogis around me. Later, when I read *The Return of the King*, by Tolkien, I realized it was like the hobbits returning to the Shire after all their adventures with Gandalf and Aragorn. It was the air of confidence that they exuded, not so much the other characteristics. They had been around. They knew some of the ropes of the outside world. They were coming back to help save their people from this plague that had come upon them. I got a glimpse, although brief, of what could happen with a few committed, knowledgeable men in this Kogi tribe.

Chad informed me that he had Cabu Ortega and a police car waiting in San Pedro to evacuate the sickest people. All of a sudden, everyone seemed to get much better except for Cecilia and Gloria. I believe Josafina also came with us with her sick baby. By the time we got to Ciénaga, it was dark, and the police decided we had to stop for the night. They took us to a third-rate motel. This is the only time in Colombia that I have had to sleep on a bare mattress with no sheet, wondering how many people before me had slept on that same bare mattress and what kind of hygiene they practiced. The bathroom facilities were the most primitive I have experienced in civilization. Chad's remark was, "There is something especially disgusting about civilized filth."

In Santa Marta the next morning Chad checked us into a medium-priced hotel in Santa Marta. I carefully explained the bathroom facilities to five-year old Cecilia and two-year old Gloria. Of course Gloria was used to flush toilets in Bogotá and Lomalinda, but I was really worried that Cecilia, who was having her first trip to civilization, would embarrass me. Later, in a store Cecilia pulled on my skirt, "Gladulja, Gladulja," she insisted.

To my horror, Gloria had lifted her skirt, pulled down her underpants, and made a puddle in the middle of the floor. I completed my purchase and left as soon as possible.

I found I had trouble talking Spanish to the salespeople. I didn't think I knew much Kogi, but when I opened my mouth to say something to the people in the store, Kogi came out. Chad took the girls and Josafina's baby to the doctor to be examined. He prescribed for them and also gave us tips on how to treat all the other sick people in the tribe who had this respiratory infection.

I asked about getting a bag of the promised powdered milk from C.A.R.E. for the sick people and babies in the tribe. I was told that it had arrived but had to be kept in the police bodega (warehouse) until a lot of paperwork was finished, so we had to return to Santiago's farm with only the few cans of the expensive powdered milk that we could afford to buy.

About this time, a young engaged couple joined us in our tribal location. They were considering working with the neighboring Arhuaco tribe. During Easter vacation, Chad, Hugh, Santiago, and Chaddy made a survey trip to scout out the opportunities in the Arhuaco tribe. Santiago told us that his tío (uncle) lived in Mamarongo. This tío was a mama to the Arhuacos and would guide them up over the ridge into Serancua, an Arhuaco village. He would also be the interpreter as he knew both Kogi and Arhuaco.

It was wonderful to have both Russell and Sharon home with me for a week as well as Marty, the girl who was planning to marry Hugh. I packed Chaddy a change of clothes in a plastic bag and watched him head down the trail with the others. I hoped it was not a mistake to send a nine-year-old on an arduous trip that would stagger many an adult man.

The Arhuacos were culturally similar to the Kogis, but there were some very important differences. They spoke a related but mutually unintelligible language. They were larger and more aggressive than the Kogis. They also had their own special clothing, white but in a slightly different style. Their hair was also worn long, both men and women. The men wore a distinctive beehive-shaped hat made of fique fiber.

Some of the Arhuacos had adapted "civilized" dress. Others worked in blue jeans on their farms, and kept their special white tribal dress for going to town. They also used coca leaves in much the same way as the Kogis. Their religion was similar, but according to Santiago, they were not as strict as the Kogis. They didn't have enough mamas so they had to rely on Kogi mamas such as Santiago's uncle, Mama Dzimata in Mamarongo.

Details of this trip are told in *High Adventure in Colombia*. Suffice it to say that Chaddy returned after eleven days on the trail with his clean clothes still in the plastic bag. He had carefully carried them all the way, but never put them on. The soles of his stockings were completely worn out inside his rubber boots. He had made the trip just fine. In fact Chad gave him the credit for saving Hugh and him from being lost in the mountains. Hugh was delayed at a stream, putting on his boots after cooling his feet in the water. He took a wrong turn as the trail was very dimly marked. After a while Chad missed him and went back to look. He found Hugh, but now they were both lost. Meanwhile Chaddy kept up with the Indians, and marked the trail so that Chad could follow. Chad was very proud of him and thought he had the most capable nine-year-old in the world.

Chapter 15

A Horsy Tale

One morning during a time when Amanda, Gloria, and I were alone in the tribe, a Kogi couple came to visit. They were from a Kogi village a little less than halfway between Santiago's farm and Mamarongo. The man introduced himself in Spanish as Mariano. They had come to get Chad to go home with them to treat Mariano's mother who was ill. They were very disappointed to find that he was not at home. It seemed that Chad had given the old woman a parasite treatment for stomach pains as he passed through their village between Mamarongo and our home, but she was not any better. It seemed like she could not eat or evacuate properly. I was afraid that maybe she had a bowel obstruction caused by a ball of worms. We had learned about that possibility in the lectures at Jungle Camp. I wasn't too sure what to do about it, but I felt that I should at least go to see her.

I had never gone away and left Gloria with Amanda before, and neither had I traveled alone with the Indians. Amanda was willing to stay alone with Gloria. She encouraged me by assuring me that there would only be one large, dangerous river to cross. She knew a rum peddler who lived right near the river crossing. His family owned a horse with long legs that could make the crossing without getting me wet. She was pretty sure they would loan me the horse to get across the river.

I soon had my gear together, and we started out. Mariano carried my things in a large Kogi mochila. Mariano knew quite a bit of Spanish and seemed to be quite knowledgeable and gentlemanly, so I felt safe about going with them. The first place we reached was Amanda's family home. Señora Raquel was very surprised that I was traveling alone with the Indians. She invited me in and made me a snack of coffee and fried plátanos. Then she wanted to see my lunch and was quite shocked to hear I didn't have one. (Now I knew why Amanda had insisted that I stop to visit her mother.) She searched around until she found a large glass jar that had formerly contained instant coffee. She broke off a chunk of panela of a size that would fit in the jar. She told me to fill the jar with water at every stream, shake the jar to mix some panela into the water, and then drink all the water. She assured me that this would give me lots of energy for the trail. Then she gave me a big plastic bag of hard-boiled eggs.

About an hour further down the trail we came to the rum peddler's house. Before the days of drug runners and guerrillas, rum peddlers were the persona non grata in the mountains. They took homemade rum to the Kogi villages where the Kogis would trade it for their chickens and pigs, and sometimes even their cooking pots. These rum peddlers were usually also guaqueros or grave robbers. They could sell any beads, golden figures, etc. they might find as pre-Colombian artifacts. This trade was illegal of course, but they seemed to get away with it. I really didn't want to have anything to do with such an unsavory character, but I had to get across the river somehow.

We found that the rum peddler was not at home, but his wife gave us a good welcome and was willing to have me use the horse. Since I was returning the next day, she said I should take the horse along with us on the trip to the Kogi village and use it to get back across the river again. I crossed the river without mishap. It was very deep in the middle, and it was a good thing the horse had extra-long legs. A very primitive bridge made of two long, slender poles stretched high above the river, and that was how Mariano and his wife crossed. It was almost like walking a tightrope, but there was a pole for each foot.

From the river to Mariano's house, the trail was uphill almost all the way. At first I stayed on the horse, but he did not want to climb the mountain. Mariano said the horse was reluctant to leave his home and pasture and would get better the farther we went. He cut a long switch and swatted the horse around the hindquarters. As long as Mariano was behind with the switch, the horse would keep moving, but he was getting slower and slower, and at last he could go no farther. His breathing was heavy, and his sides heaved in and out with each breath. He was covered with sweat. Mariano helped me dismount, and after that, I had to walk. Mariano or I had to walk behind the horse with the menacing switch, making special sucking noises that are used in that area to keep mules and horses going. The horse was so slow that we all wished he were back home in his pasture. I usually have trouble on uphill climbs, but that horse set such a slow pace, I wasn't even winded. At each stream we stopped. The Kogis drank water, and I followed Señora Raquel's instructions with the jar and panela. I shared the hard-boiled eggs with the Kogis. Mariano ruminated his coca, and his wife nursed the baby, then we would continue.

About 4:30 p.m., we arrived at Mariano's place. They brought the old woman out into the light in the patio in front of the houses, so I could examine her. I gave her medicine, prayed for her, and even took her into the woods a little ways and tried an enema, but there were no results. I told Mariano he would probably have to get help and carry her in a hammock down to the plains for medical treatment. Darkness had fallen, so they carried my things into another house, and hung up my hammock. The wife stirred up the fire, and Mariano lit some crude lanterns made by tightly twisting a piece of cloth as a wick into a bottle of kerosene. (Our boys tried this once using white gas instead of kerosene and almost burned down our house.)

The wife fried some plátanos and scrambled an egg for me. The rest of the family ate boiled root vegetables and green bananas out of a common pot. A bark mat was placed near the fire for the wife and baby, and Mariano brought in another hammock that he hung for himself. (Usually the Kogi man sleeps in a house apart.) It didn't seem to me that the couple slept much at all that night. They had a small radio tuned to a Spanish station and listened to music and conversed until long after I had dozed off.

At 3:00 a.m. they woke me up. They seemed very excited. They brought the little radio over near my hammock. To my surprise, there was Theodore Epp and the *Back to the Bible* broadcast. It was in English, and there I was in the middle of Kogiland, high in the mountainous jungle, listening to this well-known American preacher. I was familiar with Pastor Epp. My mother listened to his programs regularly as I was growing up, and he had visited our church when we lived in Grand Rapids, Minnesota. Chad had even had the honor of going fishing with him.

Mariano was very pleased to have found a program in English for his American guest. By the time the half-hour program was finished, the wife had the morning tinto ready. This was strong black coffee, sweetened with panela. They gave me the one enameled cup, and the rest of them shared a hollow half of a gourd. Once again the Kogis ate root vegetables from the common pot, and I was given fried plátanos and a fried egg on the one plate in the household.

By the time we were finished eating, the first morning light was creeping over the mountains. I went to see the old woman again who lived with some grandchildren in a nearby house. She seemed perkier than the day before, but my meds had not produced the desired result, I was told. I stressed the need for them to take her for medical help if the problem continued.

Now rays of sunlight were breaking through the leaves of the trees. Mariano had the horse saddled. The horse seemed to be in better shape than he had been the day before, and the trail was going to be mostly downhill. The wife swung the baby onto her back by the head strap and with the mochila she was making in hand, started down the trail. Her nimble fingers would not miss a stitch, even while her bare feet trotted along down the winding uneven trail. Mariano shouldered the large mochila with my hammock and sleeping bag. I stayed on the horse, and we passed up the streams where we had stopped on our uphill climb the day before.

When we reached the river, Mariano asked me if his wife could mount behind me on the horse. I gave consent, and he lifted her with the baby still on her back, to sit behind me on the tall horse. Then to my surprise, he jumped on the horse himself and with a shout and a slap on the rump, the horse headed out into the river. He staggered a bit in the deepest current but recovered himself and clambered up the far bank. We were across, all five of us, counting the horse.

The rum peddler's wife was happy to see us back all safe and sound. After another cup of strong, sweet coffee, we headed down the trail again, this time all of us on foot. It would be another three hours or so before we would see our little house on Santiago's farm.

After a little refreshment, Mariano and his wife thanked me for my visit, and started back to their home. I had really enjoyed their company. They seemed to be a high-caliber couple to whom I could relate better than to many of the extremely primitive Kogis. I hoped I would see them again.

Amanda and Gloria were glad to have me back. I don't remember what Amanda gave me to eat, but I hoped it wasn't fried plátanos and eggs. Soon Chad and Alfonso returned and were amazed at the story of my adventure.

We were saddened to receive the news about a week later that the horse had died. As far as I know, I was not blamed at all. It dropped dead right while the wife of the rum peddler was riding it. I think the poor creature was sick before I ever borrowed it, but I had to endure a lot of kidding from my family that it was my heavy weight that had done in the large horse. (I weighed a lot less then than I do now.)

Chapter 16

Precious Junk

The school year was drawing to a close. One day a traveler between Carmelo and Nueva America stopped to tell us that Sharon was quite sick at Carmelo. It was one of those times when Amanda had gone to visit her family, and I was just serving our noon meal when the messenger arrived. I took off down the trail within about 20 minutes with only the dog as a companion. This dog had been left behind by the before-mentioned German couple, and the missionaries at Carmelo had given her to us. She was not a small dog, just a little smaller than a German Shepherd or Labrador Retriever. (I am not a dog lover, but on a hazardous trip like this, I thought it was better to go with a dog than to go alone.)

Chad stayed at our home with Gloria and to care for several sick Indians whom we were treating. This was the first and only time I crossed the log bridge and climbed the steep slope up to San Javier on foot. (The other times I had a mule to ride.) Concern for Sharon gave me strength and courage. I did not walk on the log. I straddled it and inched myself along with my arms. Chaddy and Sharon had taught me that trick. The dog swam the river, which was not swollen. As I climbed the steep bank, over a thousand feet high, I stopped to catch my breath at the turn of every switchback. Once on top, it was just a matter of time (about three hours of winding along the jungle trail) to reach Carmelo to aid my sick daughter.

I walked as fast as I could, but when I arrived at Carmelo, Sharon had already been taken down the mountain road to the doctor in Santa Marta. I was very disappointed, but it was too late to do anything more that day. I stayed all night at Carmelo, and in the morning started my trip back to Santiago's farm. Chad would have to be the one to go to Santa Marta to see what had happened to Sharon.

(I found out later that Sharon had not been very sick. Her roommate, the only other girl in the school, had been diagnosed with hepatitis and sent home. Sharon became despondent, being the only girl in the school. The missionaries interpreted her pining look as illness and were afraid she had contracted hepatitis from her roommate. That is why they were so quick to send her to the doctor. To me, it seemed that she must be gravely ill to be sent all the way to Santa Marta so quickly.)

Early the next morning, I started home. I was quite concerned because the dog had not been given anything to eat, but I had a good breakfast with the boys in the children's home. On my way back to San Javier, I was greeted by name by a young civilizado man. He seemed to know me, although I did not remember him. He was very happy that he had run into me, and he begged me to come to his house to see his wife who was very sick. I enquired about her symptoms and decided she must have a urinary infection. I had suffered a great deal with this ailment, so I had much sympathy for the sick woman. The man seemed very believable, but I realized it was not a safe act to go off with this man to his home; however, I decided to take the risk. At least I had the dog with me. She would probably have defended me against any aggression.

At his house I found that his young wife was very sick indeed. Three small children clung to her as she sat in a chair wrapped in a shawl. She was pale, thin, cold, and obviously in pain. I don't know that I had any medicine in my Kogi mochila to give her, but I prayed for her and encouraged her as much as I could. The young husband escorted me back to the main trail. I never heard of these people again, but I do hope the Lord healed that woman. After thinking about it, I decided that he must have been at Carmelo when we passed through and therefore saw me and knew my name.

I arrived home without incident, and in the morning, Chad took off for Santa Marta. He found Sharon, who seemed to be fine. He asked her if she wanted to spend two nights in a medium-priced hotel or one night in a luxury hotel on the beach and one night in a cheap hotel. She picked the latter choice. She had a wonderful time at the beach and at the nice hotel; however, she really did get sick at the cheap hotel. It must have been the food. When Chad and Sharon got back to Carmelo, it was decided that she not return to school but spend the few days that were left of the school year with us in the tribe. I think they all realized that she was lonely. Sharon wished that she could stay in Santa Marta and live on the beach. She thought she could sleep on the sandy beach and eat fish from the vendors. We had a hard time convincing her that this was not an option.

In a short time, we all went to Carmelo to pack up the children's school things and bring the boys back to the tribe. The other parents were arriving from Barranquilla, Cartagena, and other parts of the civilized world. We arrived from the opposite direction. As we rounded a corner where our trail hit the mountain road that descended to the coast, we met a car filled with missionaries that had just come up the road from Ciénaga. I was covered with mud and leading a mule on which sat my two bedraggled daughters. My hair and face were partially hidden by a beat-up straw hat. The missionaries gave me a very polite greeting in Spanish, and by the tone of voice, I knew they mistook me for a rural woman of Colombia. I was rather pleased that I had integrated so well into the local scene, but I wondered what they would think when after I had had a shower and a change of clothes, they realized that I was the mother of their sons' classmates.

That evening, when I learned that Chaddy had earned the penmanship award for the best handwriting in his grade level and another award for being the most neat and orderly in his dormitory room, I felt like he should stay at Carmelo.

"Oh, no," he wailed. "Daddy said that if I did well here this year, he would take me back to Lomalinda."

The next morning, I made a terrible mistake. While packing up Chaddy's school clothes in his footlocker for the trip back to Lomalinda in August, I found it cluttered with what to me looked like a lot of junk. I picked it all out and threw it in the trash, thus making room for his school clothes. On the way back to our tribal home, I commented on this to Chad.

"Oh, no," he groaned. "Those were very special little electric motors with cables and pulleys. With them Chaddy could make all kinds of interesting mechanical apparatuses. He had them all packed to take back to Lomalinda."

I was so sorry. I felt very bad about the whole thing, but they looked like trash to me. Chad thought he could probably rescue them the next Wednesday when he was planning on going back to Carmelo anyway. He thought that any man would know they were important and take them out of the trash. Actually, I never heard about those motors again, but from that time on, I have not messed with any of Chaddy's treasures, even if they looked to me like junk.

Chapter 17

The First Landing

Chad, Santiago, and Alfonso continued to make trips to Mamarongo to oversee the readying of the airstrip. They also made a trip to Santa Marta and visited the governor of the department of Magdalena. When the governor asked Santiago what his tribe needed, Santiago said, "Tools." This request resulted in ten of each possible kind of tool that the Kogis use being sent in on flights of the airplane. Axes, machetes, hoes, and shovels were among the tools that were supplied. But I am getting ahead of myself in the story.

We were all excited about the prospect of the airstrip and going to live in a large Kogi population center. Santiago was the only one who was less than thrilled. We were his own special missionaries. He was willing to have Chad make trips to the other villages, but he wanted to keep us living there on his farm in the little house he had made for us. One morning, he got up early and starting making holes in our front patio. Into each hole he drove a long slender pole. When I asked him what he was doing, he told me he was building a clinic. He said he knew I was tired of having all the sick people in my kitchen, and he was making another building to house the sick people and the medicine. It didn't occur to him that he was occupying our only front patio, cutting off the light from my kitchen window, and just generally creating an eyesore.

A doctor had given Chad box after box of free samples, which had all been carried in by mule. The medicines were in Spanish, and unknown to us, so they were still packed  in boxes in the crawl space under the roof, waiting for someone who understood Spanish medicine to tell us what they were good for. At least we could move those boxes outside into Santiago's clinic, I thought.

María Elena had a lot of chickens. Perhaps since we were there with a big strong dog and a cat, the wild animals that usually carried off the Kogis' chickens and ate their eggs were discouraged from coming around. At feeding time, the space around Santiago's house seemed alive with chickens as María Elena or Cecilia scattered corn for them to eat. One day María Elena came up to our house with a large white hen. Its leg was broken, and she wondered if she should kill it for the cooking pot, or if we could fix it. Chaddy volunteered to be the doctor. He found some sticks to use as splints, maneuvered the bones into the correct alignment, and wrapped strips of cloth around the leg to hold the splints in place. The hen stayed close to our kitchen after that and slept under my worktable at night. She even laid us a few eggs. Chaddy became very attached to her and named her Guack-Guack.

One morning Chad left for Santa Marta. Tomorrow was the big day. The Helio Courier, JAARS' short-field airplane was coming up from its base in Lomalinda to inaugurate our new airstrip in Mamarongo. After meeting up with Chad, they would take off from the small strip in Ciénaga. Cabu Ortega was also on hand. There had been opposition from some of the other Kogi villages when they heard that the men of Mamarongo were building an airstrip. This necessitated many trips to Mamarongo and Santa Marta, but now all was resolved, and the plane was actually going to land.

I tuned in our tribal radio to pick up the conversation between the control tower and the pilot, as did many other translation teams scattered in the tribal areas of Colombia. A day or so before, at my scheduled radio time, I had sent a message to Chad through the radio operator at Lomalinda. Now the same radioman was in contact with the pilot as he flew towards Mamarongo. Chad was in the right front seat verbally guiding the pilot through the narrow mountain canyon of the Río de Tucarinca. Finally the pilot announced to the radio operator and to all of us listeners that he had spotted the site. "Chad is guiding me in," he announced. That must have triggered the radioman's memory that he had a message for Chad.

"Tell Chad that Pat is running out of T.P. in San Antonio. Be sure he brings some with him when he goes home." Then we heard the pilot repeat the message to Chad. I was terribly embarrassed that all our fellow missionaries were hearing that request, repeated twice.

Later Chad told me that the strip looked like a little postage stamp. "What makes you think we can get a plane in there?" the pilot asked him.

"Well, I know I could do it in my L-19," Chad replied. Chad had been an army aviator, flying short-field planes for the army.

"We're going in!" replied the pilot. "Everyone remember us!" That was the code word for pray. Because of our relationship with the government, we were not supposed to use the word "pray" on the air. Instead, we said remember, but we all knew what he meant. Amid much prayer from all over Colombia, the little airplane made its first landing in Mamarongo.

All was quiet on the ground. The pilot was used to a big welcome by the Indians when he landed in their villages, but not here in Kogiland. The men were all cowering in the big men's council house, to them the womb of the Ancient Mother, awaiting the end of the world. After a while, when nothing catastrophic happened, they started coming out to see the airplane. According to Chad, they liked it very much. I don't know how many flights were made that day, or how many passengers were in the airplane, but the pictures of the first landing show Santiago, Alfonso, and Cabu Ortega, as well as Chad and the pilot, and numerous Mamas and personages in Mamarongo.

I believe the plane then returned to Lomalinda, and Chad, Santiago, and Alfonso came home again. Chad brought the T.P., but not the much-awaited powdered milk. It had started to go bad, the police captain told him, so it had been distributed to the police officers, and some taken to poor neighborhoods in Santa Marta.

About a week later, our family packed up to start the long trip back to Lomalinda. We had found homes for all the kittens, and Chaddy carried his pet hen, Guack-Guack, in a Kogi mochila. Chad carried Gloria strapped to a backpack. After passing through Carmelo and picking up the footlockers, we continued down the steep mountain road to Santa Marta. Here Chad installed us all in the mid-priced hotel. I thought it was a very nice hotel, especially after living for months on Santiago's farm. It was a French hotel, the name was something like El Rincón Francés (the French corner), and it was run by a middle-aged French couple. I was worried about the cost and also that my children, used to living with the Kogis, would not know how to act in a nice place. For starters, I didn't know what to do with Guack-Guack.

I found a *lavadero* (a place to wash clothes by hand) on the flat roof of the hotel. It looked to me like the roof would be the place for Guack-Guack. Her broken leg had healed quite well by now. Chaddy tied her to one of the clothesline posts and scattered some corn for her to eat. I hoped the French couple wouldn't find her.

The next morning I went up to the roof and was horrified to find chicken droppings on the roof. (I don't know why that surprised me.) I got some T.P. and was trying to pick up the droppings, when the Frenchman came up on the roof. I was very embarrassed, and so was he, but for a different reason. "Madam (me) must not do this." He took over the job and cleaned up all the chicken droppings. I tried to explain that the hen was my son's pet. That was just fine with him. He didn't mind having the chicken there at all. He just didn't want me cleaning up the droppings. We were in this hotel for most of a week. The plane came up again from Lomalinda, this time with Uncle Cam Townsend aboard. Many flights were made between Ciénaga and the new airstrip carrying the tools, some of the police officers, and bags of the special high-protein flour supplied by C.A.R.E. Lots of pictures were taken. The story of these flights and Uncle Cam's close call with a poisonous snake are told in more detail in *High Adventure in Colombia*.

One day Gloria and I were flown in to see our new home. The frame of a house had been started down on one side of the airstrip. Gloria gathered some sticks and took them into one corner of the house where she stacked them neatly. When I asked her what she was doing, she said she was getting her firewood ready to build her cooking fire in her new home.

The Kogis in Mamarongo were friendly but very quiet and reserved. I remember one man who introduced himself to me as Pedro Juan. He spoke quite a bit of Spanish and seemed helpful and friendly. He reminded me of Mariano. He introduced me to his two children, Luis and María Elena, who seemed to be bright, active, intelligent children, a cut above the others who were more placid, timid, and full of parasites. I hoped that before long Luis and María Elena could go to school. When the plane went back to Lomalinda, we sent Chaddy and Guack-Guack along. The rest of us flew commercially to Bogotá, and then traveled overland to Villavicencio, where the small plane picked us up for the short flight to Lomalinda.

Prison Book Project
PO Box 592
Titusville, FL 32781

Chapter 18

Lomalinda Again

It was good to have our whole family together back at Lomalinda. The children were soon in school again. The new school buildings had been built over by the north shore of the lake in the area of Loma 3 and were quite a long ways from our new house, but the children didn't seem to mind the long walk four times a day. They didn't have a choice as there was no school bus or automobile. All we had was our red wagon, which served to pull Gloria around and to bring our groceries home from the *comisariato*, our little store on Loma 1.

We didn't have much furniture to fill our large living room and dining area, just the small table from the cabin, four chrome kitchen chairs and some benches. The three green and white webbed folding lawn chairs placed side by side served as our sofa. The red canvas folding lounge chair filled the other corner of the living room. By this time a number of missionaries had arrived whom we called "support personnel." These were individuals or families who joined Wycliffe not as linguists and translators, but to do other necessary tasks, thus freeing up the translation teams to go back and forth to their tribal areas collecting data and then analyzing the information back at Lomalinda with the help of linguistic consultants and various kinds of workshops. Some of these new folks were teachers, nurses, secretaries, carpenters, mechanics, administrators, parents for the children's home, radio operators and technician, pilots and airplane mechanics. The radio and airplane personnel, in addition to being Wycliffe members, were also members of JAARS

Alfonso was with us again, and we always needed activities to fill up his time while Chad was studying and analyzing the language. This latter activity took a lot longer than the time when Alfonso was actively giving him new language material. Yet it was very important to have a native speaker at hand when the need arose to check something. I had been giving him school lessons every day, but since he was not catching on very quickly, there was just so much time he could spend on this, mostly copying words into a notebook and doing simple math. The two of us still had a huge problem in communication.

After 5:00 p.m. every day, when the work day ended, Chad went to work on finishing the house. Alfonso became quite adept at helping him with this. In view of our need for more furniture, Chad decided that each boy, including Alfonso, should build himself a bed. He took them over to the carpentry shop where each one managed to make himself a simple bed. Each one was a standard twin-sized bed and nicely finished using local cedar wood that they sanded and varnished. Chad then bought each one a comfortable foam mattress. Alfonso finished his bed first as he had some time to work in the daytime when the other boys were in school. He became such a good carpenter that he went on to make me a beautiful large dining room table and a set of dining room chairs. Later, in due time, he made a living room sofa and a comfortable chair. Alfonso made the wooden frames from a plan drawn up by Chad, and we completed the project with large squares of foam, covered with a vinyl material. This furniture served us well for at least 25 years, and now, some fifty years later, we are still using the dining room table at our house in San Martin.

Amanda had come with us to Lomalinda this time. She wanted to earn some money so that she could start Bible school at Carmelo the next year. She and Sharon inherited the bunk beds after the boys had finished their single beds, and the folding aluminum cot became Gloria's place to sleep. Amanda was a great help to me, especially with the cooking, and she also joined Olga in the ministry to the local country people who lived around Lomalinda. The local congregation of Spanish-speaking people continued to grow. The story of the beginnings of this Christian group is told in *High Adventure in Colombia.*

In addition to the American missionary support personnel, Lomalinda had also hired some Colombian employees, and even some Indian people from other tribes to help with the ongoing work at our translation center. One of these was Emiliano Forrero, a young man from a jungle tribe. He became a very good carpenter, and I believe he also was one who helped Alfonso and our boys in their carpentry projects. I believe he was also the first one who started taking Russell and Chaddy alligator hunting at night, fishing, and taught them the jungle skills in which the jungle Indians are so expert.

In spite of all the help from the support missionaries and the Colombian employees, sometimes translators had to be drafted to fill basic personnel needs at the base. From time to time Chad was asked to act as the base coordinator, the person in charge of all the practical details of the base, Lomalinda. Another person, always a translator, was named tribal and technical studies coordinator and was in charge of the linguistic work and tribal teams. Both of these men worked under and reported to the branch director whom we elected every two years at the annual conference. An elected executive committee made the rules to govern our behavior and assisted the director. This of course is just a glimpse of how our branch of the Wycliffe Bible Translators was governed.

I believe that it was at this time, the fall of 1967, that Chad was asked to take the responsibility of base coordinator. This meant that we had to stay at Lomalinda during these months. I was happy to be there with all of my children together in our new house, and I tried to keep working on the Kogi language with Alfonso.

We had dismantled the water tower at the cabin and moved all the barrels to the new house. When I found time to go through the contents of the barrels, I was disappointed to find that all the hand-me-down clothes that my sister Dorothe, had sent us in 1965 were now too small for Russell and Chaddy. Gloria could wear some of the girls' clothes that had been passed down by her cousin, Becky; however, many of these were also too small. Besides these clothes, I also had all the baby clothes that Gloria never did wear because she spent six months in a body cast. Sharon had outgrown clothes as well as had Chaddy and Russell, so I had quite an assortment of used children's clothing on hand. I decided to visit our Colombian neighbors to see how many children were in each family.

After 5:00 p.m., when the work day ended, I started visiting the Colombian homes that had been built along the road between Lomalinda and the town of Puerto Lleras, 5 kilometers away. Many were on little hilltops overlooking Lomalinda. Most of them were made of mud with thatched roofs, similar to the houses of the Kogis but were square or rectangular instead of round. Many of these people were now attending the little church in the area and were friendly to us North Americans. They were the families of the children who used to come to see us and ask for a cup of cold water. The mothers were happy to point out which children were theirs, and I carefully noticed their sizes. Then I sorted the used clothes and made a bag for each family.

The neighbors were delighted with their bags of clothing. Besides the fact that they were so poor, it meant a lot to them that someone from the gringo community cared enough about them to visit them in their homes and inquire about their families. From my viewpoint, I was delighted that I could communicate with these people using the simple Spanish I had learned from Santiago and María Elena. Some of them came to visit us, bringing their children dressed in the clothes I had given them.

November 3 was Chad's fortieth birthday. He was two and a half years older than I and also older than many of our close friends, so his going into a new decade of life was always a traumatic event. It never seemed to be such a big event when I got to the new decade myself. He decided to have a party and told me to invite all the older people on the base. Chad and I were about ten years older than most of the other translation couples who had come right to Colombia after finishing their college education. However, there were some older couples, several who had moved on to their second translation, or were in Colombia as linguistic consultants. Others were there as support people. Several had started their tribal work in Ecuador or Peru and moved into Colombia to continue with the same language group. I invited all of the above-mentioned as well as several younger couples who were special friends of ours.

It was an exceptionally successful party. I had asked the people to bring small humorous gifts of little monetary value. Much ingenuity had been used in coming up with these gifts. The only one I can remember now was a little plastic paratrooper, complete with a small parachute to commemorate Chad's days as a paratrooper in the US Army. Chad was not very diplomatic in those days (later after working with Uncle Cam and others, he became very diplomatic), and he ended up throwing a damper on the whole event. After the refreshments, when the guests were gathering up their belongings and saying good-bye, he made an announcement. "I suppose you all wonder why you were invited to this party. Well, it is because Patty thinks you look like you are 'over the hill.'" There wasn't much I could do to offset that remark.

About two weeks later, a letter from home brought very sad news. My brother Darrell had died accidently while duck hunting. The accident took place on the very day of Chad's fortieth birthday. Of course this was devastating news. To my knowledge Darrell had not been walking with the Lord since his early teenage years.

I was saddened that my family had not contacted me immediately. In those days we did not make many long-distance phone calls, and we certainly had never called another country. I learned later that they did not want me to spend the money on a ticket home, but I felt left out and excluded from being with them in this time of sorrow. I suppose they felt that I was emotionally distanced from them and did not feel it was important for me to be with them. By the time I got the news, the funeral had been over for almost two weeks. I had secretly harbored a plan to bring Darrell to Colombia for a visit someday. I thought that here he would see a different way of life. Now that would never happen. It was too late.

I grieved for him and the rest of the family. He left behind a wife and three little boys.

We were due for furlough in the summer of 1968, and that was less than a year away.

Chapter 19

Christmas 1967

The time passed quickly, and soon it was December again. At the time of the conference just before Christmas, Chad's time of service as base coordinator would be over, and we could be off to the tribe again, this time to live at our new location in the village of Mamarongo. In January, Amanda would return to her home in the mountains to prepare for Bible school, and Chad and I, together with Alfonso, Gloria, and Chaddy would travel to the Kogi village of Mamarongo. Russell and Sharon would stay in the new children's home with the houseparents, Dan and Rosie Doyle, who had arrived from California with their four children to fill this position.

This would be our fourth Christmas in Colombia. The first one was a simple affair in our little temporary one-room cabin with only our immediate family and Alba. The second one must have been the same, as it was so uneventful it has slipped from my memory. The third was in our tribal location near Santiago's house with our Colombian neighbors, Luis and Josefina, Amanda, and our Kogi friends. Now this year we were back at Lomalinda and were a part of a large and growing community. Christmas programs and parties were shared in English with our fellow missionaries prior to the big days, but the 24th and 25th were left free for family celebrations.

All during the weeks just prior to Christmas, a rumor spread through the missionary community. It seemed that there was a large shipment of Christmas presents in Miami that had been sent by churches and relatives. It was hoped that they would arrive before Christmas. The children became very excited as the day drew near. Would the shipment arrive in time? At first the grapevine news was that it would. The kids were all dancing around in anticipation. Santa Claus was on his way! My heart was filled with foreboding. Wasn't this the kind of commercialized Christmas that I had hoped to avoid? All the kids could think about was the big shipment of toys and gifts that was coming from Miami. Sharon and I with Amanda's help made Christmas cookies and other holiday goodies. I remembered our Colombian neighbors, the same ones to whom I had given the bags of children's clothes, with a plate of homemade Christmas treats for each family.

I also had another fear concerning the expected shipment from Miami: What if it arrived and there was nothing for our children? I could not imagine any of the grandparents buying presents, wrapping them, and shipping them to Miami. Then the word passed from family to family that the gifts would not arrive in time for Christmas. We could expect them after New Year's Day. Of course the disappointment was great, but I was rather relieved. Chad and I had provided the usual simple gifts, one for each person.

The gringos had reserved Christmas Eve and Christmas Day for traditional family activities, but not the Christian Colombians. These country people whose homes were very impoverished had nothing special to look forward to on these days of holiday. The normal celebration was to scrape together funds to buy a bottle of wine or something stronger and a tin of store-bought cookies. This would be their Christmas cheer. The Christians however, jubilant in their new-found faith, announced a church Christmas program on Christmas Eve. Amanda was very active in the little church, and from what I gathered from her, it was going to be a very special celebration. Our family, as one of those who reached out in friendship to the Colombian Christians, was especially invited.

I was very happy about this invitation, but when I told Chad and the children, I found out that none of the rest of my family shared my enthusiasm. They wanted to spend Christmas Eve the way we always had done, at home with just our family. I can't imagine that I left my family on Christmas Eve and went to the Spanish Christmas program, but it seems that I did. Maybe I talked them into all going, but they came home early; I don't remember.

What I do remember was that the Colombian program turned out to be a tremendous production. Amanda played the part of the Virgin Mary with the life-like baby doll we had given Sharon for Christmas two years before as the baby Jesus. All the characters were there: shepherds, angels, and wise men. The dialog was good, and the costumes were tremendous. Most of them were made of brightly-colored satin material.

Our Colombian friends had put their hearts into this program, and it came off far better than I would have ever expected. A few other missionaries had also broken with tradition and left their families to attend the program, and we all agreed that this drama needed to be repeated for all the missionaries to see. We decided to talk to the leadership at Lomalinda to arrange for a repeat performance in the dining hall/tabernacle building for everyone.

When Amanda and I returned to our house after the Christmas program, what a sight met our eyes. The shipment had arrived. There were gifts for the Stendal children. My sister Dorothe and her family had bought and gift-wrapped two or three gifts for each one of us. The children were hyper. Each one had a new toy that had come out since we had left the United States almost three years before. There were beautiful dresses for each of the girls made of the first perma-press material that we had ever seen. I was kind of disappointed that my family hadn't waited with the gift opening until I returned from the Spanish service, but I guess that was too much to expect.

Chapter 20

Into the New Year

In early January we started out to accomplish the ambitious plans we had made together with our immediate superior, Tribal and Technical Studies Coordinator Al Wheeler. The Kogi tribe was one of three related tribes in the Sierra Nevada de Santa Marta. Hugh and Marty Tracy, the engaged couple who had visited us when we lived at Santiago's place, were now married and were ready to enter their chosen tribe, the Arhuacos. Chad had been asked to "allocate" them.

This meant that he would go to the tribe with them, help them make friends with the people, and make sure they had a place to live and a person to help them learn the language. Usually a missionary who was already working with a similar tribe in the area would be the "allocator." In this case, it was Chad.

The situation was complicated by the fact that we, Chad and I, were also going to a new tribal location. I knew it would be a lot different for us to live in a large Kogi population center rather than with just four or five Kogi families. I felt like we needed someone to allocate us as well.

Another complication was that all of us were operating on very limited funds. We had to plan this whole thing very carefully to make it work. By now our Colombian branch of Wycliffe had our own short-field airplane, a Helio Courier called The Friendship of Indiana. It would be a long flight to bring it from the eastern plains of Lomalinda to the mountains of northern Colombia, but the airplane was vital to carry us from Ciénaga, the nearest airstrip on the northern coastal plains into the mountains to the little postage-stamp-sized airstrip Chad and the Kogis had built at the site that for several years we would call Mamarongo, the place of the Mama.

In those days, Chad was filled with a lot of vim, vigor, and vitality, and was tremendously optimistic. With the help of all concerned, especially me, he was usually able to carry off his ambitious plans. One day I complained to some older missionary women from the Mexico branch, "It takes me working night and day to carry off all Chad's plans." "That's okay," one of them answered. "It takes all of Wycliffe working night and day to carry off all of Uncle Cam Townsend's plans."

One of the cardinal rules of public relations that Chad learned by working closely with Uncle Cam was that when entering a new region, one should always call upon the important leaders of the area, both political and religious, to make friends, tell them what we were planning to do in the area of their jurisdiction, and make sure that in a crunch they would be on our side. Chad had already made friends with the governor of the department in connection with the Kogi work, but now an additional challenge presented itself. The Catholic Church was very strong in the Arhuaco tribe, and Chad felt we needed to visit the bishop and make friends. This was quite a challenge for four Protestant missionaries.

Leaving Alfonso and Chaddy and as much of the gear as possible to come up in the Helio Courier, Chad and I with three-year-old Gloria, and Hugh and Marty Tracy, met in a town on the eastern side of the Sierra Nevada to make friends with the bishop. Chad had already laid some groundwork. He found out that the bishop was an avid stamp collector, so he visited all the missionaries in the area and got them to donate stamps

to the project. This had the desired effect on the bishop, and he invited all of us into the mountains to a famous Catholic mission station among the Arhuacos. A special meeting had been planned, and the president-elect of Colombia would be attending.

Chad had also made friends with a lawyer-type of person, to go along as our guide and had rented a jeep for the trip. I got to sit in the front seat with Gloria on my lap beside the lawyer, who was driving the vehicle, as we started up the steep mountain road. This time we were on the opposite side of the mountains from Carmelo. It was noticeably much drier country with less vegetation.

When the lawyer found out that Hugh and Marty were newlyweds, he wouldn't stop making jokes at their expense. He kept telling them that now they were in their *"luna de miel"* (Spanish for honeymoon), but that next would come their *"luna de hiel,"* and he would laugh and laugh. We knew what luna de miel meant, but we didn't understand what was so funny about the rest of it. The lawyer knew a little English, and when everyone else got out of the car, he told me that hiel meant gall, and then he kept repeating his joke and laughing as we bumped along up the mountain road.

All the rest of the passengers except Gloria and I were jammed into the back of the jeep, sitting sideways and bumping their heads on the roof of the jeep as we bumped along. They were getting very tired of the lawyer and his joke. I was at least trying to chuckle to be polite, so the lawyer seized another occasion to explain to me that first came the luna de miel when they were all happy as Hugh and Marty were right then, but later would come the luna de hiel, the time of bitterness, when the baby came and kept them up all night. Then he laughed again uproariously at his joke. Hugh and Marty didn't think it was funny and developed quite an aversion to our guide.

At last we arrived at the mission station. It consisted of some impressive-looking buildings of a Spanish-mission style. On the way up we had come across the president-elect and his party who had descended from their vehicle and were looking at the scenery. Chad jumped out and introduced himself and Hugh and Marty. The president-to-be was just friendly enough to keep from being impolite in the presence of his associates. When we arrived at the mission station, we found out to Chad's disappointment that the bishop had not yet arrived. The lawyer introduced us to several nuns who seemed to be running the mission. We received a reserved welcome and were ushered into their reception room where the one who appeared to be the Mother Superior poured us each a small glass of wine.

There we sat, four very uncomfortable Protestant missionaries who had each signed a statement promising to abstain from all alcoholic beverages and cigarettes as a condition of joining the mission. In our Jungle Camp training we had been taught to always accept an offer of hospitality, even if you thought a cup of strong black coffee might kill you, but no one had said anything about wine. When one after another we refused the proffered wine, the nuns' token of hospitality, the Mother Superior looked like she couldn't believe it. The lawyer solved the problem by quaffing down all five servings, but you could see by the look on the nuns' faces that now they were sure that Protestants were just as bad as or worse than they had suspected.

We asked if they could give us a place to spend the night, and a sister grudgingly showed us to a room. In it we found two cot-sized beds. At first we thought the room was for one couple and that we would be soon shown another room for the other couple, but that didn't happen. All five of us had to sleep in these two small beds. Hugh and Marty gallantly offered us the slightly larger of the two since we had Gloria to sleep with too. Chad and I actually got some sleep. In the morning we found that Gloria had wiggled up and stretched out across the top of the bed above our heads, but Hugh and Marty found out that there was no way they could both lie in that narrow bed at once. I believe they took turns.

Before they showed us to the room, we were offered a very slim supper, and the next morning someone hit Chad up for an offering to cover our stay. In spite of our meager resources, Chad pulled out a generous bill from his pocket. That changed the atmosphere, and an order was given to make us an excellent breakfast. After that we attended a mass in the mission chapel. Outside of the orphans who were being housed at the mission and a few lay workers, attendance was poor. We noted that few if any of the Arhuacos passed forward to receive the host.

At some point during the morning, the bishop arrived, and a few speeches were made. The place where the Tracys were going to be allocated was on the other side of the mountain in a remote Arhuaco village across a ridge from where we would be in Mamarongo. It seemed that it was not considered to be a threat to the mission to have some Protestant linguists way over on the other side of the Arhuaco area.

Chapter 21

In His Steps

During Easter vacation of 1967, Chad and Hugh, accompanied by Santiago, Alfonso, and Chaddy, had traveled to Serancua, the village where Hugh and Marty would be living with the Arhuacos. They had not found any spot in the rugged terrain where an airplane could land, so the prospective translators would have to travel to the village on foot. The Tracys shipped their tribal gear overland to Aracataca, a town at the foot of the mountains on the western side. It would be a three-day mule trip from Aracataca to the Ahruaco village of Serancua.

Considering the logistics before us, there were two possibilities to choose between. One option was for Marty to wait in Aracataca while the rest of us met the Wycliffe plane in Ciénaga, a town near the mountains between Santa Marta and Aracataca. The plane would shuttle us all, together with the Stendal tribal gear to the newly made airstrip in Mamarongo. The men would spend a few days getting me set up in our new tribal location among the Kogis, then Hugh and Chad would climb the ridge to Serancua, an arduous one-day trip. When they had found a place for the Tracys to live, Hugh and Chad would rent some mules and go down the mountain to Aracataca, a three-day trip, and then bring Marty and the goods back up, another three-day trip. Then after Chad saw that the Tracys were doing all right in Serancua, he could come back to the children and me in Mamarongo.

The problem with this scenario was that Marty would have to stay alone in Aracataca a week or ten days, maybe longer. This would be expensive, lonely, and probably not even safe. I would be without Chad for a long time in Mamarongo. Neither Marty nor I were very happy with this plan, although in hindsight, it may have been the better of the two choices.

The other plan started with us all shuttling to Mamarongo. After a few days setting up our place, Hugh and Chad would make the trip to Serancua, find a place for the new translators to live, and possibly send some Arhuacos with mules down to Aracataca to get the Tracys' tribal gear. Then they would come back over the ridge to Mamarongo to get Marty and take her over the ridge to Serancua. When Chad saw that they were doing well, he would come back to Mamarongo.

If the choice were yours, which plan would you choose? Neither Marty nor I had seen the trail between Mamarongo and Serancua. It was a difficult, rugged, seldom-used trail, we were told, but it could be traversed by anyone who could do it at all in one day. Chaddy had made the trip with the men when he was only nine, but he was back at Lomalinda in school when the present plans were being made. I was secretly hoping for the second option. It would be nice to have Marty's company there in our new location in Mamarongo for a while, especially while the men would be gone.

Ultimately, the choice was left to Marty. She thought it all over and decided she would rather have one very hard day on the trail rather than the long days of waiting alone in Aracataca and then the three-day trip to Serancua, even if they could get a mule for her to ride.

After attending the meeting at San Sabastian, the four of us took a plane to Santa Marta via Barranquilla. Somehow I came down with another malaria attack somewhere between Valledupar and Barranquilla. The kindly flight attendants let me recline in my seat while the plane was being cleaned and fueled instead of getting off with the other passengers. In Santa Marta Chad found an inexpensive hotel-apartment right on the waterfront. (Yes, the one with the faded green sofa.)

The Wycliffe airplane arrived on schedule from its base at Lomalinda, bringing Chaddy and Alfonso as well as our tribal gear. The next morning, I was still too sick to travel, so it was decided that the pilot would make a flight with Chaddy, Alfonso, and part of the tribal gear. The second flight would be Hugh, Marty, and Chad. Gloria and I would be left for the third flight the next morning. This would give me one more day to recover. The story of the next few days is told in Minnesota Mom, Volume I, *Beginnings*. Suffice

it to say here that the plane's radio went on the blink right after leaving Chaddy and Alfonso and some of our gear in Mamarongo. It took four days in Barranquilla before the radio was fixed. After I recovered from the shock of knowing that my ten-year-old son had been left in Mamarongo, I concentrated on getting well, and by the time the plane returned, I was over the malaria attack.

After landing on the short airstrip (a thrill in itself), I found that the house lacked a bit in the way of finishing. Chad had had sheets of tin roofing flown in the previous summer and inexperienced hands had done the roofing. It looked kind of weird with sheets of tin going in all directions, but it was watertight. (A close call with fire in the thatched-roofed house in San Javier had made Chad decide to roof this one with tin from the beginning.) This house was a little larger than our house on Santiago's farm, and not quite so tall. The walls were made of mud and a mud wall divided the interior into two rooms, the kitchen and the bedroom. A fire on the floor in the corner of the kitchen would be my stove, and we hung up hammocks wall to wall in the bedroom.

Chaddy and Alfonso were distressed as they had set up a racetrack in the dirt floor of the bedroom, and raced little battery-operated cars with flashing lights, much to the amusement of the Kogi men. Now we had trampled all over their racetrack, and our clothes and hammocks filled all the space.

Chad must have flown in some lumber, and very soon we had some benches to sit on in the kitchen and the same kitchen table that had served us so well in our Lomalinda cabin. Marty and I unpacked the kitchen gear and the food supplies and organized it all into some semblance of order; we had both been to Jungle Camp. Each visiting Kogi family brought a hand (stalk) of bananas, a mochila of yuca, malanga, or arracatcha, or some other locally grown vegetable.

We soon noticed that one man seemed to be in charge of us. He was always right outside our house, machete in hand. If we left the house, he watched us carefully. We were told his name, and we thought it sounded like Bruhilio, so that is what we called him. Later we realized that the Kogis were trying to say Virgilio (Virgil). Still, we think of him as Bruhilio. We were allowed to go to the stream for water and to walk on the airstrip with no problem, but if we veered off in another direction, he was right there to ask us where we were going and why. These questions were given in simple Spanish with a very authoritative tone. Alfonso told us that he was the village cabu (Spanish for corporal; in English we would just say policeman). He was in charge of us, and we had to have a good reason to wander away from the airstrip. We were used to the authoritative manner of Santiago, so we were not offended. The only good reason to leave the airstrip seemed to be to treat a sick person. Marty was able to make him understand that she needed to have exercise in order to build up endurance for her coming

trip to Serancua and thereby gained a little more freedom. (Chaddy and Alfonso were exempted from this restriction. It seemed like they had been accepted as being harmless before the rest of us arrived.)

In a few days, Chad and Hugh were ready to leave for Serancua. Accompanying them as their guide would be Santiago's uncle, an interesting Kogi man who served as a mama to the Arhuaco tribe. He had also been their guide and interpreter on the previous trip that Chad and Hugh had made to Serancua. Mama Dimata was uncle's name, but we just called him tío (uncle).

Before Chad left, he made a study table and bench for Chaddy. There was no room for it inside the house, so he set it just outside up against the wall and under the overhang of the roof. Here Chaddy was supposed to be doing his fifth grade schoolwork. His nemesis was long division. Both Alfonso and Chaddy stayed with us women in Mamarongo. They had been to Serancua before, and I don't think either of them had any desire to make that trip a second time. Chaddy was very surprised to think that Marty was planning to take the route over the ridge to the Arhuaco village. He told her all about it, stressing that it was extremely steep, rugged, and tiring. "Someone once tried to take a burro over that trail," he told her, "and the bones of the burro are still up there. Next there are going to be Marty bones up there."

Marty and I had a good time while the men were gone, inventing meals that could be made with our limited supplies and kitchen facilities. I continued ministering to the sick who came every day, just as I had back at Santiago's place, and to my great relief, they all got better. Once in the middle of the night, a man came seeking help for his wife who was very ill. They lived some distance away, but since Chad was not there, I felt that I would have to go. From the husband's description, I decided that the woman must have pneumonia, so I packed the appropriate medicine, including a penicillin shot, in a mochila, donned my sturdy tennis shoes, grabbed a walking stick, and started out.

To my great relief, Alfonso woke up and decided to go along. It was a very black night with no moonlight. Alfonso found two strong flashlights, one for each of us. He followed the man and told me to keep my light right on his boots and come right behind him. Off we went, uphill and down, in and out. I concentrated on putting my feet in Alfonso's footsteps. We were in the heart of the dry season, so the trail was not particularly muddy.

Finally we arrived at our destination, and I decided that the woman indeed did have pneumonia, or something very close to it. I gave her some pills, injected her with the penicillin shot (amid much prayer), and then we retraced our steps. Once again, in the thick darkness, I concentrated on Alfonso's boots, putting my feet exactly in his steps. At last we arrived home, and I gratefully climbed into my hammock for a few more hours of sleep before it would be morning.

Just below the small level area where the airstrip, our house, and the beginnings of a small village were located was the confluence of two rivers. The Kogis build very unique bridges. Rocks, mud, and large logs are used to build an approach on each side of the river. The middle part is spanned by one long medium-sized pole, well supported by the two approaches. Two slightly thinner poles serve as handrails. The whole thing is woven into a V shape, using smaller poles and vines. Just below the village were two of these bridges, making foot travel possible without crossing through the raging rivers. Since we had flown in by airplane, I had only seen these bridges from a distance. They were picturesque, but they did not look very safe, and I decided that I would never have enough nerve to cross a river by using one.

The next morning at breakfast, I asked Alfonso where we had been in the middle of the night. "Oh, up that hill," he said, waving his hand to indicate the other side of the river. "Not over the bridge!" I hollered. Alfonso just sat there stoically and gravely nodded his head in the affirmative. I couldn't believe it! I had actually crossed that bridge, not once, but twice in the thick darkness. I would have been scared out of my wits to do it again in the daylight. Later in the day, as I pondered the event, I realized there was a spiritual application. We can do a lot of things we wouldn't think possible, if we just keep our eyes on the Lord and follow one step at a time.

Later in the day, the husband of the sick woman arrived. He reported that she was much improved, and Alfonso was willing to go and give a second penicillin shot. He had never given a shot before, but I gave him instructions and prepared the injection for him, slipping it back into the sterile wrapper until he was ready to use it. (Thank the Lord for disposable needles and syringes instead of the glass ones we had to sterilize and use in Jungle Camp.)

Chapter 22

Mariana Arrives

Marty and Chaddy continued their hikes. One day Marty told me that they had visited the farm where the old woman lived whose healing had resulted in our permission to use the airstrip. Her name was Marta, the same as Marty's. She sent me a gift, a very well-made miniature mochila containing two eggs, and a verbal message with Marty that she would soon be coming to visit me.

The men had accomplished much during their few days in Mamarongo before they left for Serancua. They had built me a work table down one side of the kitchen with a shelf underneath for storing items such as pots and pans. They had also built shelves above the work table for dishes and medical supplies; however, one item that had not been built was a door. The kitchen area had two openings, one on each side, and a very cold wind swept through the kitchen in the afternoons, chilling me to the bone. Jose Gabriel was very attentive after the men left, but even though I told him in simple Spanish that I needed a door, he did not seem to get the picture.

When we lived by Santiago near San Javier, Chad recorded many Kogi phrases on a large reel-to-reel tape recorder, and we played them over and over, hoping that some of the language would stick in our heads. A serious complication to language learning was that the language possessed many morphophonemic changes. In languages such as Spanish or English, if you know a number of vocabulary words, you could usually string them together into an intelligible sentence. Not so with Kogi. All we could do was memorize long sentences. If we tried to change one word, the required morphophonemic changes made the whole thing unintelligible, or at least it seemed. I realize now that the last thing that Santiago wanted was for us to start talking Kogi. If that happened, his life would not be worth much. He taught us a few useful phrases and then hoped we would be satisfied with that.

Now with my need for a door, I reached back in my mind for something I had learned by listening to those tapes. I knew the word for door. It was a hard one to pronounce and had a heavy nasal sound. But how could I say, "I need"? Finally I remembered what I thought was the verb for need from one of the tapes, but I didn't know how to put the whole thing together in a sentence. I thought for a long time, and I finally thought I had a sentence together; however, the first-person part was an area subject to morphophonemic changes. I finally decided it could be said one of two ways. The next time Jose Gabriel showed up, I tried it out on him, saying it first one way and then the other, repeatedly. He didn't seem to respond, but the next morning he showed up with a huge heavy door made of boards painstakingly chopped from a tree trunk with a primitive axe. Somehow he installed it into the empty space that had been left for a doorway. It opened and shut just fine, swinging on large wooden pegs. He must have understood that I really needed a door.

The old woman, Marta, turned out to be a very gracious person, the first Kogi I had met who seemed to have a touch of that we might call "social graces." She may have once lived among non-Indian people, or perhaps the older generation of Kogis had been a bit more polished in their manners. She knew a little Spanish and with the Kogi I had learned while living with Santiago, we were able to communicate somewhat. She brought me a second small mochila containing an egg and a small bunch of long onions from her garden. I had learned from Santiago the correct way to receive such a special gift. I sniffed the onions for a while and exclaimed over them using the correct term, which I later learned meant, I like it, or I want it.

Instead of the fearful, sullen look that we had come to expect from first-time visitors, Marta's wrinkled face was all smiles, and she seemed to genuinely accept me as a friend although it was our first meeting. Even the mere fact that she had a well-established Spanish name set her apart from other older Kogi women. She made me understand that she was Jose Gabriel's mother. He was our closest neighbor and the one who had built our house on his land. He was also one of the three Kogi men who had come to Santiago's house and invited Chad to come to Mamarongo and show the men how to build the airstrip.

After a few days, Chad and Hugh returned. All was going well, they reported. They still had friends in Serancua. Sick people had been treated and all recovered. Some of the sick who had been marvelously healed during their first trip in 1967 remembered them and were very grateful. One girl and her mother sought Chad out to bring him a special lunch, which included a hard-boiled egg and a bottle of brown sugar water mixed with milk. The daughter had been restored from a coma during the first trip, and now the girl was completely normal.

Hugh and Marty had been offered the use of what Chad considered to be the best house in the village, and a group of Arhuaco men with mules had been sent down to Aracataca to bring back the Tracys' belongings. Everything should be there by the time the Tracys and Chad returned to Serancua.

Marty felt strong and ready for the journey, so the Tracys and Chad soon left for the trip up the mountain and over the ridge to their new home among the Arhuaco Indians. These Indians, while related to the Kogis, spoke a language that was mutually unintelligible. Physically, they were stronger and taller than the Kogis, and their culture seemed more advanced. They made more use of horses and mules, and were more aggressive in their relationships with the dominant Latin culture of the region. Quite a few of them were fluent in Spanish, and they were well-known in Bogotá where they were not shy about showing up to demand their rights from the Colombian government. This was in contrast with the Kogis who for the most part were shy and retiring and felt quite intimidated by the national government.

We were told that the Arhuacos were not as serious about the Indian religion as the Kogis, and their mamas were dying out. That was why Santiago's uncle, Mama Dimata, although a Kogi, functioned as a mama for the Arhuacos.

The next weekend after Chad had left with Marty and Hugh, I was deluged with visitors. They brought so much food in the form of yuca, plantains, and other produce from their farms, that I didn't know what to do with it. Jose Gabriel suggested that as the hostess of the house, I was supposed to cook up a large quantity and serve it to the visitors for lunch. I must have looked dismayed, so he said he would send his wife, María Antonia, to help me.

At that time, my "stove" was a fire on the floor in the corner of the kitchen. A large open space above the mud wall and under the roof allowed the smoke to escape. I tried to keep the fire going, and at night, I banked it with ashes heaped over the last coals and charcoal so that I wouldn't have a hard time starting it again in the morning. This usually worked.

Since women are not allowed to carry firewood in the Kogi tribe, Chaddy and Alfonso were the wood carriers and kept me in a good supply. We were at between 3,500 and 4,000 feet of altitude, but to the southeast rose up the peaks of the Sierra Nevada de Santa Marta, the highest of which reached almost 20,000 feet, so the afternoons and nights were chilly when the wind blew down off the frigid heights. Only from about noon to 2:00 pm did the heat from the fire in the kitchen cause any discomfiture and that only on the rare day when no rain was falling during that time.

The main problem with feeding so many people was the job of peeling all of these foodstuffs. I was not experienced with this activity, and it took me a long time. Another factor was that the peeling of the green plantains exuded a sticky white sap. It was hard to wash off, and if not removed promptly, it stained your hands black. Most Kogi woman bore the marks of this sap on their palms and fingers. I wanted to identify with the women of the tribe, but I really didn't want this sap on my fingers.

I possessed four cooking pots of various sizes which nested together for travel and storage. I had to plan carefully in order to utilize these aluminum pots, each with a strong wire handle and cover, to best advantage to feed a multitude of people. Each one had to be carefully balanced in the fire on rocks or pieces of firewood, so that they would not tip and spill their contents into the fire. One of the wisest purchases I ever made was a very large teakettle made of very heavy aluminum with an immense flat base. This teakettle when filled and kept at the boiling point supplied instant hot water for my many cooking needs. Carrying water was now my job, but in this location a small stream, located only a stone's throw from the house, supplied my kitchen needs. The only problem that presented was that I was not allowed to dip the water from the stream with a metal utensil. Public opinion had it that so doing would cause the stream to go dry. Jose Gabriel furnished me with a very dirty-looking large half gourd with which to scoop the water from the stream into my aluminum bucket. When I suggested using a piece of my plastic Tupperware instead, he agreed that that would probably not cause the stream to dry up since it was not made of metal.

María Antonia came up and was a great help peeling enough of the *bastementos*, as they are called in Spanish, to fill my larger kettles. I was able to successfully feed all the visitors and minister to their varied ailments. Santiago had made a point of teaching me the vocabulary needed to attend the sick. The Kogis had a great time visiting among themselves and looking at the pictures in the *National Geographic* magazines we had brought. We also had several View Master 3-dimensional viewers with reels of pictures of interesting animals and beautiful mountain scenery. We had flown in a number of large jars of Nescafe and tins of store-bought cookies, so I served steaming cups of instant coffee, thanks to my ever-ready supply of hot water in the large teakettle, and two cookies to each visitor. I wondered what to do about the children; I had been firmly taught in the United States that children should not drink coffee. We thought it would stunt their growth; however, in Colombia, especially in the country, all of the children drank coffee. (Chaddy and Russell were happy to walk the half-hour trail to Luis and Josefina's house when we were living with Santiago in order to come home and report that they had each consumed a large cup of strong, sweet black coffee.) These Kogi people were so short anyway, that I certainly didn't want to be the one to stunt their growth even more, but neither did I want to deny them hospitality. I finally decided to give each child a *tinto* cup (a small cup) of milk flavored with a very small amount of sweetened Nescafe along with their cookie. We had learned from living with Santiago to bring in a large sack (100 pounds) of powdered milk.

María Antonia was such a big help that I asked Jose Gabriel if I could hire a woman to help me in the kitchen. (I was hoping he might volunteer his wife.) He said he would take it up in the men's council meeting that was to be held that night. However, on Monday morning he informed me that all the men had decided that Kogi women could not work outside of their own families. That seemed to put an end to that idea. (I realized later that the women do most of the weeding and routine farm work.) I resigned myself to not having a kitchen helper. To my surprise, on Tuesday morning a Kogi man arrived with his small daughter in tow. The girl was beaming from ear to ear and her father announced that his daughter wanted to be my helper. "Whatever could she do?" was my first thought. She was just a little taller than my three-year-old Gloria.

The man's name was Francisco Gil. I had seen him on some of the pictures taken by Hugh Tracy and Chad on their first trip to Serancua by way of Mamarongo in April. He was a son-in-law to Old Marta. The girl was Mariana, the oldest of five daughters. She was not as young as she looked. Since her mother was Mercedes, the sister of Jose Gabriel, he was her uncle. It would be proper according to Kogi custom for her to sleep in his women's house with María Antonia and spend her daytime hours with us. Mariana's family lived together with Old Marta about half an hour's walk from our house. And so began our relationship with this very interesting family. Who could guess what an important part they would play in our future?

I was very happy to see Pedro Juan again. He came to visit often, bringing several members of his family each time. It seemed that he had two wives. Catelina, the older wife, also knew quite a bit of Spanish. She introduced me to her two children, Luis and María Elena. These two were also the children of Pedro Juan, and I had met them when Pedro Juan brought them to see the airplane before. They were probably between ten and twelve years of age. They also knew some Spanish and seemed to me to be smart and knowledgeable, above the status of other Kogi children their ages. Once again I hoped that they would be able to go to school before too long.

On another occasion Catelina came to visit bringing a grown-up daughter, María Louisa. It seemed that María Louisa was also a wife of Pedro Juan, obviously not his daughter. She had a number of small sons, younger than Luis and María Elena. They too seemed to be alert and intelligent, not dull and placid like many of the Kogi children. It seemed strange to me that such a capable, somewhat acculturated man as was Pedro Juan would have a second wife, the daughter of his main wife by a previous husband, but I later learned that this arrangement was not at all uncommon among the Kogis.

Santiago had made a big point of assuring us that he did not approve of plural marriage—one woman at a time was enough trouble in his opinion. Long before we had met anyone from the Mamarongo area, and Santiago was trying to make arrangements for us to be welcomed in Don Diego, he assured me that I would never want to go to Mamarongo. "They don't eat salt there, and they marry little young girls to old, old men," he told me.

Chapter 23

A Kogi Madonna

While Chad was still gone, Santiago made his appearance. He had made the three-day overland trip from his home near San Javier to visit us in our new location. Chad had told me that Santiago had the function of *abogado*, or lawyer/judge, in the tribe, and now I began to understand what that meant.

Santiago was a very "take-charge" person. In spite of his small size (4 ft. 6 in.), he demanded respect and exercised leadership among the other Kogi men, who were generally more timid and retiring. As soon as Santiago's presence in the village was known, a meeting was appointed for the next weekend in the men's council house. Kogis, both men and women, started making their way to our house, hoping to catch Santiago in a mood to hear their side of some current dispute. At the weekend meeting, Santiago would hear both sides of complaints, render a decision, and extract a fine or penalty from the person judged to be in the wrong. The leadership of the area, the mamas, and the inspector, a civil position appointed by the Colombian officials in the town holding jurisdiction over that particular area of the mountains, would take part, but I believe the final judgment was made by the abogado, a person from outside the area. I was later horrified to learn that the fines imposed went into the mochila of the abogado.

The value of the system lay in the fact that unpopular decisions would be made by the outside abogado who would then leave the area and not have to rub shoulders with the person who lost the decision. Santiago was just the person to swagger into the area, listen to the complaints, render the decisions, and return to his home, his ego somewhat inflated, and his mochila a little heavier from the experience.

Women were at a disadvantage during these meetings, as they were not allowed to enter the men's council house. This house was quite a bit larger than the normal Kogi house. It was warmed and lighted by four fires since the meetings were held at night. The council house was considered to represent the womb of the Ancient Mother. No woman was allowed to enter. A "sergeant at arms" stood just outside one of the two doors. He was one of the *cabus*, policemen. Women who had a part in the matter being discussed were allowed to gather just outside the door. The cabu acted like a speaker system. He repeated to the woman the gist of what was being said inside. If she had anything to say, she told the cabo, and he repeated it to the men gathered inside. The men sat in the cozy warmth and mellow light of the interior while the woman stood outside in the dark, shivering in the icy wind that whistled down from the snow-covered heights above the village. I was warned by Santiago to stay away from the men's council house. Should I or any woman step inside, the whole building had to be burned. Such was the jealously of the Ancient Mother. She must be first in the hearts and minds of the Kogi men.

Because of that, a number of women made their way to my kitchen in the days immediately before the important meetings. I especially remember one, a twenty-something mother with a year-old child at her breast. High cheekbones and regular features glowed in the candlelight illuminating her face as she earnestly pled her case. Santiago sat at my kitchen table, his face impassive as he sipped the strong black sweetened coffee I had served him after dinner. The cup of coffee I had given the woman sat forgotten as she earnestly poured out her heart in what to me seemed like beautiful, poetic Kogi, or Kougian, as they call their own language. I longed to understand what was being related. I could only catch a familiar word here and there, although I felt she was making a serious charge against her husband. Santiago uttered a nasal affirmative from time to time to encourage her that he was listening. How I wished I could capture on camera film the drama before me. The woman with her child looked like a beautiful Madonna in an artist's painting. Everyone else had wandered away to pursue other activities, but the three of us (four with the child) seemed caught up into a capsule of candlelit time, remote from the rest of the world.

My heart went out to this woman. Could I believe that Santiago would give her a fair judgment? Actually, that was not too likely. His judgments were not shaped by God's law. He had probably never heard of the Ten Commandments upon which our Judeo-Christian law system is built. His judgment would be made based on the ancient myths that had been passed down by word of mouth from generation to generation, and probably influenced by who would be able to "line his mochila with silver," not likely to be this woman. As I sat there, I poured my heart out in prayer for her, that justice would be served, and that most of all she would come to know as Lord and Savior, that one who always had a place in His heart for hurting and abused womanhood.

The candle burned down, and it was time to seek our hammocks. I determined to try to find out the identity of this woman and follow her case as best I could.

I did find out that this woman was named María Teresa. She was a daughter of Old Marta and sister to Mercedes and Jose Gabriel. In contrast to Mercedes, who had experienced a stable marriage with Francisco Gil, María Louisa's life had been rocky. She did not live near enough so that I saw her often, but every once in a while she appeared, usually because of a sick child who responded to prayer and to our treatment. I had observed that she was the second wife of one of the prominent Kogi men. After the judgment by Santiago, she seemed to become kind of a shirttail second wife to the younger brother of the above-mentioned man who was the father of her children. Her younger children claimed the younger brother as their father. Her beauty gradually faded as the years took their toll.

Imagine my delight some forty years later to see her now-wrinkled face in the congregation of the Christians together with two of her granddaughters. Her nephew, not yet born at the time of the above story, assured me of María Teresa's Christian faith and praised the Christian character of the oldest granddaughter who was one of only three Kogi girls attending the school where he is the Christian teacher. It has taken a long time, but individuals are being snatched away from the bondage of the Ancient Mother, one soul at a time.

Now nine years later, we received word that Teresa was the second Kogi person to pass on and receive a Christian burial. Others may have died in the faith but were buried in

the traditional pagan manner by their relatives. Teresa was an avowed Christian and her children were in agreement that she be buried as a Christian. Another of her nephews, the Kogi pastor of the Christians, wrote to me that his Aunt Teresa reminded him of Anna in the account of Luke 2. I look forward to seeing Teresa again one day around the throne in the great throng that no man can number.

Chapter 24

Spiritual Opposition

Beginning about the time that Chad and the Tracys left for Serancua, I began sensing a spirit of oppression. I can only say that as I lay in my hammock at night, I felt that evil, opposing forces were closing in on me. It seemed as though a voice was saying to me, "You can't stay here any longer, this is my territory. I am in control here." As I started to physically tremble, another voice would be heard, "But you have to stay here. This is MY call on your life. This is why you went through all the previous years of preparation. You are needed here." It seemed as though the "conflict of the ages" was raging in my soul. In spite of the cold, clutching fear that permeated my heart, I would try to resist the evil and choose the good voice. Finally I would drift into a troubled sleep.

In the cool mist of the dim morning light, as I left my hammock to build up the fire and start the day's activities, this oppressive fear would be driven into the background of my mind. I don't remember mentioning it to anyone until many years later. When I did, Chad said he had never experienced this sensation; however, both of my daughters, Sharon and Gloria, knew exactly what I was talking about.

It is true that I was needed there. After our breakfast of oatmeal or pancakes, the visitors would start arriving.

Bruhilio and his family were usually first. As Mrs. B. took up her post on the bench by the door and received her cup of sweetened Nescafe, she would tell and show me her children's health problems. The scalps of many of the young children in this area were covered with sores. These were nasty, pussy things, and as we found out, very difficult to cure. The B. family's toddler was no exception. The first step was the obvious—a bath and shampoo with nice warm water, heated

by my fire in the corner. I would wash all the layers of snot off his face, the caked-on food as well, and then try to squeeze out as much puss from the head sores as possible. After disinfecting the scalp as best I could with a solution of hydrogen peroxide, sulfa powder was liberally applied to the sores. Clean clothes were needed, so Chaddy donated one of his tee shirts. I finally got to the little tyke's feet, and that was when I really got a jolt.

I personally had been the only member of our Jungle Camp class to experience a *nigua*. This is a miserable little insect that somehow gets under the skin of a person's foot. It lays eggs that develop in a little transparent sack. This sack lies firmly attached to your foot or toe, just under the skin. A dark spot marks the place where the insect entered. Walking becomes increasingly painful. When I found that I could hardly walk anymore, I went to the Advanced Base Clinic where one of the older staff women diagnosed the problem and removed the nigua with a sterile needle. Believe me, this is not as easy as it sounds. First you squeeze the affected part with your free hand, and then with the needle, you start picking away at the skin surrounding the black spot. Skill comes with practice, and as you carefully pick away more skin, the little transparent sack of black eggs is uncovered. Of course you are disinfecting everything as you proceed. Now comes the tricky part. Since the sack is very securely attached to the foot, you have to carefully and patiently pick at it with the needle until little by little it breaks away from the flesh of your foot. You must not pierce the little sack; it has to come out whole so that more eggs will not be released back into your foot. I only had one, a big one, and my instructor worked on it for about 20 minutes, showing me and

 explaining all the time what she was doing. Had I not had that experience, I would have had no idea what to do with the B. family's toddler. Both feet were covered with niguas.

I sterilized a needle, and before I was done, I had dug 25 niguas out of his feet, 15 from one small toe. Sometime during the treatment, I remembered a bottle of Infastress that I had brought along for just such an occasion. A spoonful of this medicine calmed the poor child down enough to finish the job. But what was I to do with the little bare feet that were now full of holes? I couldn't let him loose to walk around through the dirt and mud. I covered the holes with sterile gauze and wrapped his feet firmly with strips of old white sheets. Then I thought of Gloria's second pair of tennis shoes. Although his feet were much smaller than hers, with all the bandage materials, the shoes were just right. In a week or so, the little feet were completely healed.

I wish I could say the same about the head sores. Most children his age were in the same condition. These sores were very resistant and difficult to heal. They may have been aggravated by head lice infestation. The Kogis did not seem to mind if the hair of these very small children was cut, so sometimes we had to cut the hair close to the scalp, and later we learned to treat for head lice infestations.

One day as Mrs. B. was showing me something on the body of her baby, I noticed big, round red circles, the scars left by sores that had healed. These covered the body and legs of the little five-month-old boy. "What caused all these sores?" I asked her.

The Kogis don't use a separate word for "bite"; they just say "eat." "The cockroaches ate him," was her reply. I am sure my mouth must have dropped open in shock. "But we eat the cockroaches," she quickly added, as though that made things even. I assume she meant killing them by biting them.

A Kogi man came for treatment for a bad injury on his foot. The cut was infected, and black dirt was caked into the gaping sore. I brought a basin of warm water and tried to get him to soak his foot. He thought I wanted it washed, and tried to wash the foot by dipping water on it with his hand. I had a terrible time trying to get him to place his foot in the warm water and let it soak. I finally got the injury cleaned and disinfected to my satisfaction, applied antibiotic ointment, and bandaged it. I was wondering what to do to keep it clean, when Alfonso, who was observing the situation, offered to give the man his old pair of tennis shoes. This act on Alfonso's part really warmed my heart. It was the first time I saw a Kogi doing a completely unselfish act. It encouraged me that the Holy Spirit was really working in Alfonso.

Alfonso was not very happy in this new location. He was from Don Diego, a village far over the mountains. His people had a traditional dislike for the people in Mamarongo. He confided to me that the only ones he felt good about here were *Bruhilio* and his family. *Bruhilio* was somewhat related to Alfonso on his mother's side. Alfonso and Chaddy stuck together.

One day I was surprised and delighted by a visit from María Ester and her stepmother Margarita. These two women had been our neighbors over by Santiago's house before they sold their farm and moved away, and it was like meeting long-lost friends or relatives again. María Ester knew quite a bit of the simple Spanish used by Santiago and María Elena, and I could communicate with her quite well. Their story is told in *High Adventure in Colombia.* (María Elena had formerly been married to Inocencio, the present husband of Margarita and father of María Ester. When we met them at Santiago's place, this family had three little girls, very close in age—Tomasa and Cecilia were the children of Inocencio and María Elena, and Patricia was the daughter of Margarita by a former marriage. Santiago went to the civil authorities in San Pedro and forced Inocencio to give Cecilia, the youngest, to her mother, María Elena.)

In addition to two-year-old Francisca, María Ester now had a baby boy, Joaquin. Margarita had her one-year-old, Rosalba. Tomasa accompanied the two women and their babies, but Patricia was conspicuous by her absence. When I asked about her, María Ester explained that Patricia was too sick to accompany them. I offered to go to their house to see Patricia. After getting permission from our guard, we started out. Surprisingly, I don't seem to remember anything about the trip, but when we arrived, I was horrified to find that Patricia had been placed up on a shelf above the fire where blocks of *panela* (brown sugar) are usually kept as the smoke helps to protect them from the cockroaches. At the time of my visit, the fire was out, and Patricia was lifted down from her perch. María Ester explained that they couldn't leave her down on the earthen floor as she would eat ashes and charcoal from the fire. (The Kogis' experience has showed them that when a person gets to the stage of malnutrition that they start craving ashes and charcoal, they do not live long, so they try to physically restrain them from eating these things.)

I was appalled at the change in Patricia from the time I last saw her. She had been a healthy, lively little girl like Tomasa, probably about six years old. Now she was an ashen skeleton without strength to play or even walk. Her swollen face was a pasty yellow color. In those days we tackled malnutrition with a vengeance. I suspected hookworm, a parasite that enters through bare feet in contact with worm-infested soil. I arranged for Patricia to have a treatment for parasites. The next step was nutrition. In the 1950s in the USA a coarse powder was developed called Multipurpose Food. It was supposed to provide all the nutrients necessary for life. The only required addition to a diet of Multipurpose Food was a calorie source—candy bars and peanut butter were suggestions. People purchased this to have on hand in case of atomic attack, etc. We had brought a case of six large cans with us to Colombia, and one was with us in Mamarongo. I made a mixture of this Multipurpose Food powder, raw oatmeal, powdered milk, and shaved panela, with a little bit of white sugar to make sure the mixture was appealing in taste. This mix could be eaten dry (like the 'snuff we made for survival in Jungle Camp) or cooked like porridge. I think a child like Patricia would just put some in the palm of her hand and lick it. I also gave her a bottle of liquid multivitamins. With this treatment, Patricia recovered, started eating normal Kogi food again, and the last I heard of her, she was a grown, married woman living in another village. On the other hand, little Tomasa died sometime during the time that we were in the USA on our first furlough. I was told that the illness that took her life was vomiting and diarrhea. She must have dehydrated.

Chapter 25

Whose Will All This Be?

Time passed, and Chad did not return. Meanwhile I worked out a system of cooking, washing dishes, washing clothes, taking care of Gloria, and attending the visitors, mostly sick people with ailments. Washing the clothes was the biggest problem. Mr. and Mrs. B. continued to come every day. Jose Gabriel must have decided that he could just as well put our guard to work since he had to hang around our house every day. Bruhilio started framing a small Kogi house next door to us on the uphill side. I was told that was going to be the new home of María Antonia. It was interesting to watch the progress of the Kogi construction.

Mrs. B. continued to take up her accustomed place on a bench just inside our door. She was very involved in everything that happened. She looked at all the pictures in the *National Geographic* magazine and became adept at using the View Masters. She observed everything that went on inside the house, and hopefully she gave a good report to her husband. Once she realized that Mariana was helping me in the house, Mrs. B. wanted her son, Valencio, to help as well.

Mariana was expert at tending the fire and preparing the local bastementos for cooking. She really liked our food and was ready to help with anything that furthered the preparation of our meals. Once she got the idea that we couldn't eat again until all the dishes from the last meal were washed, sterilized, dried, and put away, she was ready to pitch in to help with that chore. Since she was too short to reach the dishpan when it was placed on the kitchen table, I put it on a low bench for her, and Mariana was able to wash all the dishes in warm, soapy water and place them in another dishpan where I scalded them with boiling water from my trusty teakettle, dried them with a clean dish towel, and put them in the cupboard. I was very careful to follow all the sanitary precautions we had been taught in Jungle Camp. All the sick people in the entire area were making a beeline for our front door, bringing their disease germs with them.

Mariana's family, the family of the Old Marta, seemed to me to be a step up on the social scale from the other people in the area. They were fairly clean in their appearance, and Mariana especially bathed and changed her clothes often. I began to consider her to be a part of the family. Sometimes, especially in the evenings if I was tired, I let her dry the dishes with my clean, sanitary dish towel. I kept a different towel made of terry cloth for drying hands and other uses. (At Jungle Camp we had been taught to make a tripod of three poles to hold an aluminum washbasin for hand washing, and the hand towel hung from the top of one of the crossed poles.) One evening I was horrified to see Valencio helping Mariana dry the dishes using the hand towel which was also falling all over the front of his absolutely filthy garment. I didn't want to offend Mrs. B., so I told her that drying the dishes was girls' work and that I would give Valencio some boys' work to do.

Chad had brought several aluminum containers of different sizes with very tight-fitting lids. These were used in rural Colombia as milk containers, but at Santiago's house, we had found them very useful for carrying water over the rugged up-and-downhill terrain as the close-fitting lid kept the water from spilling out even when it was jostled. The next morning, I chose a milk pail about the right size for Valencio and gave him the task of carrying water from the river for washing the clothes. (He was young enough so that it was culturally acceptable for him to carry water. Alfonso was now pretty much past that age.)

In addition to the hand-washing basin and the two dishpans, I also had two larger plastic tubs for clothes washing. I filled one of these with water that Valencio brought me, added powdered laundry soap, and let our dirty light-colored clothes soak in the soapy water while I attended the morning visitors and Mariana washed the breakfast dishes. Later, I found time to agitate these clothes with my hands, wring them, and place them in the second plastic tub, which by this time contained another bucket of the water brought by Valencio. I found that a little vinegar added to this second tub of water helped to remove the soap. Then I filled the first tub with our darker-colored clothes using the same soapy water. Later on, I would have the kitchen benches full of Kogis of different ages working on reading-readiness activities while I ran from the laundry tubs to the dishpan to dry the breakfast dishes, dispensed medicine to the sick, served instant coffee to all the visitors, and then with Mariana's help started lunch

When I felt the first load of laundry had been in the rinse water long enough, I wrung the garments out by hand and pinned them to the clothesline that Alfonso put up for me on the downhill side of the house. By doing a little laundry every day, I was able to keep ahead of it and never had a huge pile of dirty clothes. Chaddy and Alfonso washed their own clothes down at the river. Chaddy also insisted on washing any large items like Chad's trousers, hammocks, blankets, or large towels. He and Alfonso dunked them in the river, one garment at a time, laid them on a long, flat rock, and rubbed them with strong, blue bar soap. Then they swirled the garment over their head and slapped it on the rock. The sound reverberated up and down the canyon and sounded to me, the mom from Minnesota, like beavers slapping their tails in the water.

Before I developed the above system for laundry, I took all our dirty clothes in a plastic bag down to the river accompanied by Gloria. As had happened before when we lived with Santiago, Gloria fell into the river, but once again, she was on the upstream side, and the swift current swept her within my reach. As I struggled up the steep embankment with dripping Gloria in one arm and the plastic bag full of the heavy wet laundry slung over my shoulder, I vowed to never try to wash in the river again.

As had happened with María Elena, Santiago's wife, Mariana wanted no part of helping with the laundry. To her, we were washing clothes that were not even dirty.

Finally one day, Chad returned. He was very thin, tired, and dirty. He had been on the trail for 19 days. He confirmed that Marty had made the trip over the trail to Serancua, but it had been much harder than she had anticipated. Chad and Hugh had to help her over one very steep part with small climbing ropes that they had brought along. (Chaddy was amazed that she had made it at all.) A disappointment awaited them when they arrived at the village. Although a group of Ahruaco men with mules had gone down to Aracataca on the plain, the policemen where the Tracys' belongings were stored would not release the cargo to them. They had made the three-day trip back up the mountain empty handed.

Instead of coming right back to his family in Mamarongo, Chad had to borrow some mules and go down to Aracataca to bring back the supplies while Hugh stayed in Serancua with Marty who could not be left there alone. It took about a week for Chad to make the trip down, get the cargo released, and bring it all back up the mountain. In the meantime Hugh and Marty had to stay in Serancua with very inadequate supplies as their sleeping bags, food, cooking utensils, etc. were all in the baggage that had been left in Aracataca. Finally Chad returned with the cargo and helped them get set up in their new home. Then, at long last, he was able to come back to us in Mamarongo. I had forgotten to bring a mirror when we flew in to our tribal location in Mamarongo, and I was very surprised and amazed that Chad had remembered to buy a small wall mirror in Aracataca and had carried it with him all the way to Serancua and then on to Mamarongo without breaking it.

The next morning Chad woke up not feeling well. This seemed to be understandable in view of the exhausting trip he had just experienced. However, a day of rest did not do the trick. The next day he was worse and started running a fever. I searched the medical book for some disease that fit his symptoms. As he kept getting worse instead of better and did not respond to any of our simpler medications, I decided to try an injection of Aralen. That was the malaria medicine that had saved me when we lived by Santiago. In spite of the injection, he just got worse and worse. Our Kogi neighbors didn't know what to think. Here was the great healer who had brought their chief back from the brink of the grave, and he couldn't heal himself.

I really got worried when Chad had me call Chaddy to his bedside. I realized that he was in a sense saying good-bye to Chaddy and telling him that he didn't know what was going to become of him without a father to keep him in line and give him his spankings when he needed them. I realized that Chad thought he was dying, so I got the two-way radio into action and tried calling Lomalinda. We were so far away from the base that communication was very difficult, especially later in the day. Our twice-a-week contacts were always made in the early morning. The radio operator heard my call and understood that I wanted to speak with the nurse. Soon she was on the line. After I explained the situation to her, she decided that Chad must have malaria. I objected, saying that I had already tried giving him the injection of

Aralen, and it hadn't helped. When she understood that the injection had been 1 cc, she told me that was far too little. I should have given him 3 cc every six hours until he started getting better. Fortunately, I had quite a few injections of Aralen in our medical supplies, so I was able to give him the recommended dosage. It took a while, but slowly he started to respond to the medicine and our desperate prayers.

During the worst part of Chad's illness, our guard Bruhilio came in to visit him. I guess Chad looked pretty sick as he lay there in his hammock. Bruhilio looked at him for a while and then mustered together his meager Spanish and asked, "If you die, whose will all these things be?" These words were accompanied by a sweep of his hand that included our hammocks and sleeping bags, the kitchen equipment of kettles, dishes, etc. Then we realized that though to us we were living with the barest minimum necessities, to our neighbors, we were wealthy beyond imagination.

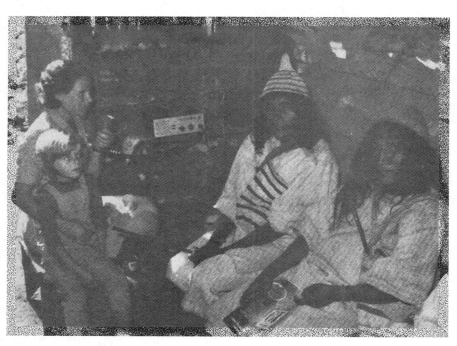

Chapter 26

Life Continues

Chad eventually regained his strength, and in the meantime I continued my daily routine. I forgot to mention that I was also supervising Chaddy's fifth grade studies. Chaddy was having a wonderful time. He had found a baby wild turkey, and it became his constant companion. As he studied, it sat beside his math book on his wooden desk out under the overhanging roof of the house. He taught it to perch at night on the edge of his hammock with its backside out, thus avoiding the droppings. Chaddy and Alfonso had discovered some very interesting insects—red, white, and black butterflies with numbers on their wings. If you looked from one angle, they said 68; upside down, they said 89. People back at Lomalinda found that hard to believe. The boys also had some unique caterpillars in their hammocks. As they crawled around the hammocks after dark, red lights flashed at one end, and green lights flashed at the other.

Chaddy had always been fascinated by fire since he was a toddler. When we lived in the suburbs of Minneapolis, he seemed to almost always know and be present when any of our neighbors burned their trash. Many times he got too close and singed his eyelashes and eyebrows and sometimes even the front part of his hair. Here in Mamarongo in March, the work of the Kogi men was burning their fields to prepare them for planting. They practiced slash-and-burn farming as did many of the other Indian tribes and country people of Colombia. Medium-sized trees and brush were cut down with machetes. When the underbrush was cleared, the adult men felled the larger trees with the few axes available in the valley. This was accomplished before the start of the dry season. Now the end of the dry season was drawing near, and it was time to burn the dry brush. The larger trees would smolder a bit, but the fires would go out and these larger trees would later fuel the Kogi cooking fires. Since the jungle is very damp, there was no danger of forest fires. The problem was to get the brush to burn at all. As the North American Indians danced to bring the rain, the Kogi mamas danced to bring the dry season. The ashes left from the burning supplied important nutrients to the soil, necessary to raise a crop.

Chaddy found it very hard to keep his mind on long division while all this interesting burning was going on nearby. Chad would get the boy started on his math, but in a few minutes Chaddy would be back with the Indians who were burning the fields. One afternoon, Chad firmly seated Chaddy at his desk and told him he could not leave until he had completed his math assignment; however, in ten minutes Chad found Chaddy's seat vacant. A plume of smoke at the end of the airstrip revealed the presence of the truant. Chad grabbed Chaddy, marched him back to the house, bent him over a hammock and gave him a good swat on his backside with a ping-pong paddle brought along for this purpose. To Chad's surprise, a crackling sound followed the swat, and a small plume of smoke arose from Chaddy's jeans pocket. Chad's swat had kindled a book of matches that Chaddy was carrying in his pocket. Chaddy made a wild dash for the small stream behind our house and spent the rest of the afternoon sitting in the cool water.

Scarcely a day went by without visitors. Since all the families except Jose Gabriel's lived some distance away from our house, they would start showing up about 8:00 or 9:00 a.m. loaded with produce from their farms. The only way I could keep up with all the supply of local foodstuffs was to cook large quantities, as much as my kettles would allow, and feed everyone who was present.

Here in Mamarongo, the demand on our medicine was much higher than at Santiago's place. There were only four or sometimes five Kogi families in the San Javier area, but here at our new location, Mariana helped me identify at least 50 adult married men. After trying to develop a numerical system that became impossibly complicated, I settled on identifying the individuals by relating them to a man with a well-established and well-known Spanish name. I used well-known relationship terms in English – father, oldest son, grandson, brother-in-law, etc. Sometimes quite a string of terms was necessary to pinpoint an individual. A few women had well-established names, so they could be used too. Although the birthrate was very high (every woman was expected to produce ten babies during her childbearing years), the infant mortality was off the charts. Of the ten to thirteen babies born to a mother, she was considered fortunate if two or three lived to maturity. Allowing for the infertile people, I figured that each adult man represented a household of at least four persons. There were also men with plural wives, each wife having her own small woman's house on a small farm, the cultivation of which was her responsibility. Anyway you figured it, we had over 200 Indians in this area.

However, as at Santiago's place, the common physical ailments were repeated – respiratory infections, parasite and gastrointestinal problems, malnutrition, and arthritis or rheumatism for the older adults. A round of parasite medicine followed by vitamins or in severe malnutrition, our special mix of Multipurpose Food with our Jungle Camp-type "snuff" did the trick. We also administered a lot of first aid to both old and recent injuries. It was amazing how a little antibiotic ointment cured old infected injuries almost overnight. We had penicillin and antibiotic capsules for more serious infections, including pneumonia. We had learned by treating folks over at San Javier to treat aggressively, especially children. We tested for penicillin allergy before giving injections, but we never found a Kogi who showed the least bit of allergic reaction to the medicines or who reported any ill effects from taking our medicine. We prayed for each person and actively put our faith in the Lord to heal them. As Pastor Hegre, the main pastor at Bethany Missionary Church, always said, "Medicine can help, but only God can heal." As in San Javier, everyone who came to us got well. Toothache was common, but the only thing we could do was to give the ailing person several aspirin pills. We didn't dare give them more than a few as they might take them all at once, and we didn't want anyone to suffer from an overdose. We had the famous ipecac syrup for accidental overdoses should they occur. I don't remember if acetaminophen was out yet, but we didn't have any.

Chapter 27

Interesting Visitors

One day Mama Nacio came to visit. This was a red-letter day for me, as it was my first encounter with the famous Kogi leader. I was already well acquainted with his younger brother, also a mama, whom we called by his Spanish name, Pedro Auegi. In spite of the fact that he knew almost no Spanish, Santiago and Chad had persuaded the police inspector in Tucarinca, the Colombian town in the lowlands that had legal jurisdiction over the area wherein lay the Kogi village of Mamarongo, to appoint Pedro as inspector over the area where we were now living with the Indians. This was done at the time when some Kogis from the other side of the mountains had gotten one of their number appointed as the inspector of Mamarongo in order to prevent the inauguration of the airstrip. Pedro Auegi held this position of inspector for many, many years. He introduced himself to strangers by saying, "Nas inpector." (I'm the inspector.) Dressed in a red-and-white striped namtu (pointed chief's hat) with a red-and-white striped mochila, he cut an impressive figure. He was tall for a Kogi and had a stronger, heavier frame than his older brother. He soon became our very special friend, actually giving me a hug when greeting me, and calling me nabunzhi (my daughter).

Mama Nacio, on the other hand, was dressed completely in white, with no trace of the chubbiness that Santiago had reported previously. He seemed to be in good health. A few of the important older men of the village accompanied him. We were still quite shy about taking pictures of these important individuals, as we knew they might not understand what we were doing. Uncle Cam Townsend had loaned us his Polaroid Land Camera, and Chad snapped a shot to give the chief while I unobtrusively snapped a few pictures with our regular camera. For some reason, the day that Mama Nacio showed up, the Polaroid camera decided not to work. Chad went through all the steps three times, but no picture appeared, only blackness. Chad was sweating with nervousness, afraid that Mama Nacio would get mad, feeling that we were making fun of him or something. However, all of a sudden, serious Mama Nacio burst out laughing. He thought the failure of the picture to develop and Chad's discomfiture was hilariously funny. "That's all right," he told Chad, when he could quit laughing. "Sometimes my magic doesn't work either."

Chad took him through the routine that we always gave our visitors, listening to the testimonial tapes that our Kogi friends around Santiago's house had made, looking at animal pictures in *National Geographic* magazines, and viewing our photo album of family and friends while I prepared the cups of coffee and plates of cookies. I had been sternly warned by Santiago that the wives and children of the mamas could not have milk in their coffee or eat any beef or other product of the cow, so I was careful to not add any milk to the mama's cup. That was a mistake, as Santiago returned the cup and ordered me to add the milk. It seemed that Mama Nacio was such an important man that he could eat anything he wished. Mama Nacio was friendly but stately and showed none of the exuberance of his brother. It would be a long time before I would see him again.

On another occasion Mama Nacio's old wife came to visit. The Kogis are stoic people, not given to expressing emotion, and certainly not demonstrative with hugs and kisses as are the Latin people. However, this old woman showed affection for Chad. It seems that she also had been healed on one of Chad's early visits to the area. Now she was ailing again, so Chad gave her another round of parasite treatment and whatever else he considered appropriate. She was the mother of Margarita, Inocencio's wife, and also of our next-door neighbor, María Antonia. She had several young teenaged sons who were in seclusion, training to be mamas, and one small pale little boy about seven with toothpick-thin legs who accompanied her, named Vicente. We gave him the parasite and nutritional treatment. We prayed for all these ailing people, and trusted the Lord to touch them with His healing hand.

Santiago, as was true with Alfonso, really did not like the people of Mamarongo very much, but as he had this superior position of being their abogado (lawyer/judge) he was able to get along with them well. He especially liked Mama Dzimata (his uncle) and the two Auegi brothers, Mama Nacio and Pedro, whom he had known when he was young in the Kogi village of Palomino. Also, by his extended visit to this area, he was able to keep his hand of firm control on us, his special missionaries. Looking back down the years, Santiago was the only older Kogi who shared with us his knowledge of the history and culture of the tribe. Until the present generation of Christians, we had to figure the rest out ourselves by observation and the help of the writings of several anthropologists. While we were still living with him over by San Javier, Santiago clued us in on some of the happenings in Mamarongo, little dreaming that we would actually be living in that area someday. It seems that a dramatic tragedy had taken place. A man who was angered over what he deemed to be an unfair decision by the leadership in regards to a woman with whom he was enamored set fire to the thatched roofs and burned down all the houses in the village. This was the old village of Mamarongo, located at a higher altitude than where we were at the airstrip. The Kogis do not live at the village site, but each family has small houses on their scattered farms, one for the men and one for the women. The village is their ceremonial meeting place with a large, round men's house surrounded by small houses where the women can sleep and cook while the men have their all-night meetings. There is also a large house in the village, smaller than the men's house where women who have no family house in the village can sleep and cook.

On this occasion, the collective anger of the villagers was evoked by this destructive act. By order of Mama Patricio, an elderly mama whom I had not yet met, the arsonist was taken up to the high mountains where he was thrown over a cliff to his death. Some say his throat was slit with a machete first. This was an unusual act for the nonviolent Kogis. Normally murder or execution would be carried out by quietly giving the victim poison secretly placed in his food. However, this act of arson was not only the destruction of the village, but each family suffered the loss of whatever hammocks, blankets, animal hides, cooking pots, and clothing that they might have left in their village hut for the occasions when they met together, approximately every two weeks. These people were extremely poor by any comparison with the dominant culture, and it would take them many years to replace these items. Their only cash came from making brown sugar blocks (panela) which they might be able to sell to the non-Indian country people.

The family members and supporters of the arsonist sought justice from the Colombian governmental authorities down at the foot of the mountains, and as a result, poor old Mama Patricio was seized and carried off to prison in the very hot Colombian town of Ciénaga. It is a wonder he survived his incarceration, but at the time of our arrival to live at the airstrip, all this tragedy was a year or more in the past. At the time of Chad's first visit to minister to Mama Nacio, the burned village was in ruins, and plans were being made to rebuild it in a new location at the airstrip site. The new men's council house had already been constructed, and a slightly smaller women's house had also been built to accommodate the women who would accompany the men to their meetings. By the time we returned to live in what we then called Mamarongo, two or three individual family houses had been constructed near the two large houses.

One day while Santiago was still with us, a short stocky man with a very ruddy complexion showed up to visit us. His clothing had been mended so many times, there was more mended area than original cloth. The Kogis mend holes in their clothing by the method that my grandmother would have called darning. The hole is circled by small stitches, and then threads are added back and forth, similar to the original weaving process. We were now accustomed to the fact that many of the poorer Kogis had only one set of clothing, and so the garments are never or very rarely washed. This man's clothing seemed to be in that condition. Santiago whispered to us that this man was the "murderer," the one who carried out the order to throw the burner of the houses over the cliff. We treated him politely, but it was obvious that Santiago kept his distance. Santiago told us that public opinion forced the murderer to live in a very remote area by himself. On another occasion a very thin, malnourished-looking woman showed up with several unkempt children. This, Santiago told us, was the family of the man who had burned the houses. We were warned against getting too friendly with them. We gave them worm medicine and the polite treatment that we extended to everyone. I do not believe that any of these people returned for a second visit. It is very unusual for Kogis to resort to violence, but it seemed strange to me that the people on both sides of this tragedy were shunned by the community.

I didn't find much time to formally study the language during our weeks in Mamarongo, but I became very practiced and fluent in the vocabulary needed to treat the sick, inquire about the absent family members of the visitors, and offer hospitality. One afternoon a middle-aged woman showed up with her teenaged son. The woman was suffering from a disfiguring disease called pinta in English. First white splotches appeared on the body which in time turned purple. Over a long period of time, this disease became fatal as well as disfiguring. Chad figured out from studying Current Diagnosis and Treatment that pinta could be cured by the same treatment given for syphilis although pinta was transmitted by mosquitoes, not sexually. This treatment consisted of three powerful, long-acting penicillin shots, given at least one month apart. We had brought the aluminum cot that my mother had bought for Sharon when we left the USA for Colombia, and this was where Gloria slept. Chad liked to have patients receiving injections lie face down on the cot. I injected the women, and he injected the men. After I had given this woman her injection, I was surprised that she did not get up. This had never happened before, and I didn't know just how to deal with it. I hoped that the shot had not been so painful that she couldn't arise. After a while I offered her a cup of coffee, which she received and drank while still lying on the cot.

Hours passed, and supper time arrived. I offered the woman a plate of food, and she gladly received the meal, but she still didn't arise from the cot. The son, meanwhile, was enjoying *National Geographic* magazines in the kitchen and refused any food that I offered. He finally took a green plantain, roasted it in the fire for a long time, and then ate it. He received a glass of water after a while. Mrs. B explained that he had just come out of the seclusion of training to be a mama and was still following his restrictive diet. Darkness covered the valley, and it seemed that we were going to have these two Kogis as overnight guests. I was trying to come up with a plan so that we could leave the woman on the cot and still provide sleeping arrangements for everyone else. All of a sudden, about 8:00 p.m. the woman emerged from the bedroom, her mochila hanging from her head. She beckoned to her son, said good-bye to us, and off they went into the night. When I recovered from my surprise, I followed them outside. A beautiful full moon had come up over the top of the eastern mountain. They obviously were waiting for the moon to light the trail for them and guide them to their home. Later, we learned to cover the cot with a nylon tarp before we used it for injections. This prevented the fleas and lice that were prevalent on our visitors from finding a new home in our bedding.

Chapter 28

The Burned Baby

One day a woman showed up at our door with a little baby, not her own. In a garbled mixture of Kogi and Spanish, she made me understand that this baby had been left close to the fire all night to roast to death. This woman could not stand to be a witness to this atrocity, so leaving her own baby in the care of others, she had grabbed the burned baby and brought her to us. In fear and trepidation, I unwound the rags wrapped around the child, and there she was: a small baby, very much roasted on one side. I recognized the woman who had brought the baby and knew that this was not her own child.

The poor little mite was past the stage of cries or tears. Her little brown almond-shaped eyes seemed to plead with me for help. Although the size of a newborn, she was obviously at least three months old, if not older. One-third of her small body was covered with what I estimated to be second- and third-degree burns. Besides that, she was filthy. Her face was actually caked with black dirt from the earthen floor of the hut where she lived. The woman who had brought the baby quickly disappeared. The child was so thirsty that she reached out her little tongue and tried to get some moisture from the washcloth with which I was cleaning her face.

In spite of her injuries, this child had a tremendous will to live. Now, some 50 years later, I do not remember all the details, but I figured out some way to nourish and get some liquid into her. Probably we had brought a small baby bottle with us for an emergency such as this. I did not dare to touch the raw-looking burns with anything, but I got an idea. Just before we left the Summer Institute of Linguistics at the University of North Dakota, information was given to us on a then new product called Dermaplast. It came in an aerosol spray container, and was advertised to be the perfect treatment for burns as it disinfected, healed, formed its own bandage, and even contained an anesthetic to take away the pain. I had bought several bottles of this product and had used it once in a while on my own children's injuries with good results. I found a bottle in our bag of medicines marked First Aid Supplies. With much prayer, we sprayed all the baby's burned areas.

Santiago had returned to his home in San Javier, but in due time *Bruhilio*, our guard, came over to see what was going on. He had been made aware of the situation, and as the village policeman, he felt he should take a hand. I had the feeling that this little act of infanticide would have gone unpunished except that our presence and knowledge of the act had embarrassed the village leadership. *Bruhilio* succeeded in making me understand that the young woman who was the mother of the burned baby was about to marry Mama Nacio as his second wife. Although we had noted that certain men had plural wives, usually sisters, or sometimes a mother and her daughter by a previous marriage, we had not yet heard of the fact that important men like mamas were allowed to take a second wife when the first one got too old to bear children. The word mama in Kogi has several meanings, one of which is sun. As the moon has two stages, full and new, the mama is allowed to have two wives, an old one and a young one. *Bruhilio* explained all this to me the best he could, obviously with some embarrassment. It was implied that the young woman needed to get rid of this unwanted child by a previous relationship in order to take advantage of the wonderful opportunity of being the wife of Mama Nacio. Nevertheless, *Bruhilio* sternly assured me that the woman who had committed this crime would be duly punished.

The next day the young woman appeared, bruskly ushered into my presence by *Bruhilio*. Her punishment, he told me, was to live in my house with me for one week, helping me take care of her burned baby. She would sleep in the village, but other than that, she had to be in my house. I was not so sure I wanted this beautiful but sullen woman to live there with us, but I was left no choice in the matter. I tried to treat her kindly. I believe she nursed her baby, but she showed no emotion as to the infant's well-being. Surprisingly, the prayer and Dermaplast worked well, and by the end of the week the child was so much better that the authorities decided to send her home with her mother. I was not sure that hair would have ever grown on the burned part of her scalp, but other than that, the child had made an amazing recovery.

Our scheduled time in Mamarongo was drawing to an end. The airplane would soon be arriving from its base in Lomalinda, bringing our oldest son, Russell, and taking Chaddy back to school at Lomalinda. The plane would fly Chad, Gloria, and me to the shuttle strip in Ciénaga. It was about this time that the two birthing experiences took place, which are related in my first book in this series, *Beginnings.*

Just before the airplane was due to arrive, we received an important message from Santiago brought to us by a friend from the San Javier area. María Elena had almost died in childbirth. Luis and other Colombian neighbors had carried her out in a hammock to Carmelo, and the missionaries had taken her to the hospital in Ciénaga. Santiago was left alone with two-year-old Margot. He needed help. We were his only family. We must come at once to his aid.

Chapter 29

Back to Santiago's Place

Our time in Mamarongo was coming to an end. Tomorrow the little airplane would arrive from Lomalinda. Our guard, *Bruhilio*, came into the kitchen and announced that he wanted to talk on the tape recorder. He had been just outside our house, watching us all during our stay in the village while his wife sat on a bench in our kitchen and observed us from within. Chad set him up to record, and he gave his report. He ended his speech with the following statement: "Martin and Patricia are of God." (Of course he used the Kogi word for the highest male deity in the Kogi religious system, as far as we could figure out, a kindly, father-like figure.) We felt that we had passed a test.

The last day in the tribe, Chad and I were very busy closing up our house. It would be about a year before we could return to this little mud hut as in June it would be time for our first furlough. We would be going to the United States for several months. We packed our kitchen utensils, sleeping bags, and hammocks in 55 gallon metal drums lined in plastic where we hoped they would be safe until our return. (They were. The Kogis are noted for not stealing.)

The airplane arrived on schedule. It was good to see Russell again. It seemed like he had grown quite a bit. He certainly looked white, clean, and civilized next to Chaddy and the rest of us. Chad and I tried to make ourselves presentable to enter the outside world again. Many Kogis had arrived to see the airplane and to bid us good-bye. Our entry into their little world had been the biggest event of their (monotonous) lives. We heard one Kogi man mutter to his friend, "The older boy looks like his father, but Chaddy is a Kogi."

It was with mixed emotions that we said good-bye to our new friends who had become so dear to us during our six or eight short weeks among them. Alfonso of course went with us. He was more a member of the Stendal family than of this village. The pilot shuttled us and our luggage to the small airstrip near Ciénaga, then he and Chaddy climbed aboard the Helio Courier and started the long flight back to Lomalinda where Chaddy would finish the school year.

Russell, Alfonso, Chad, Gloria, and I climbed aboard a bus bound for the coastal city of Santa Marta about thirty minutes away. There we would restock our supplies and find a vehicle to carry us up the winding road to Carmelo, and then on down the trail to our house next door to Santiago.

We made our way to Santiago's farm as fast as we could. He welcomed us with more than usual exuberance and early the next morning he started down the trail to see what had happened to María Elena. Cecilia, who was now about six, actually did a very good job of caring for little Margot who was about two. In a few days Santiago was back with María Elena in tow. María Elena was not her former chubby self, but she had recovered well from her ordeal. She had spent a month in the hospital in Ciénaga and had recuperated enough to resume her duties as Kogi wife and mother again. The medical staff in Ciénaga had been able to save María Elena, but the infant had been dead upon arrival at the hospital, Santiago was told.

We found that all was as we had left it in our house on the ridge. Our dog had died of snakebite, we were told, and the cat had wandered off to find a better home, I imagine. As soon as Santiago had left, Louis and Josefina came over to clue us in about the emergency that had taken place. María Elena had gone into labor, but it became evident that the birth was not progressing normally. With the birth of Margot still in mind, Santiago had sought help from the neighboring civilizados. Josefina described eloquently how sad they had been to see María Elena dying in a house full of medicine. (This was in reference to the unpacked boxes of sample meds upstairs in our house and an unstated barb at us for having taken off to another village and left them to their fate. However, no amount of this medicine would have done María Elena any good, even if someone had known how to use it.) When an arm of the baby presented, the white people knew that the only chance they had of saving María Elena's life was to undertake the arduous task of carrying her in a hammock to Carmelo. Luis organized the neighbor men, and off they went. It is extremely difficult to carry a person in a hammock over these winding, steep trails. Usually only one man at a time can support the hammock on each end over these narrow trails, and they have to have quite a few men in reserve so that they can keep changing the hammock carriers. Although thin and undernourished, these country men are wiry and tough with strong lungs and legs from their arduous life in the mountains. Nevertheless it was a herculean task that Luis undertook, as even a small woman, chubby and pregnant such as María Elena was, would require a great deal of strength and expenditure of energy on the part of the men to get her to the nearest road at San Pedro, and all the while she was enduring the useless pains of childbirth, as the baby was obviously transverse and could not be born in that position.

After spending a few weeks with Santiago to make sure all was well with María Elena, we wended our way back through Carmelo, Santa Marta, Bogotá, and Villavicencio to Lomalinda. There we began to make our preparations to leave Colombia and re-enter American life, visiting our family, friends, and supporters in the homeland whom we had not seen for over four years.

By this time, we were all attached to Alfonso, and Chad could not feel comfortable about leaving him to his uncertain fate in the tribe while we were gone. After seeing that Santiago had been given poison twice, Chad was afraid that because of his close association with us, Alfonso would be killed while we were in the USA. He was fully grown now, about 5 ft. 6 in., and once we were gone, he would be required to submit to the pagan puberty ceremony, including coca addiction and sexual initiation, through which all Kogi youths were required to pass. Chad was considering attending the third session of the Summer Institute of Linguistics at Grand Forks, North Dakota, in order to earn a Masters' Degree. It would be ideal to have a real live Kogi Indian present to give examples of his own language when needed. He also thought it would be a great educational experience for Alfonso to travel not only through Colombia, but in the United States as well. We believed that Alfonso would be the first Christian and would be the teacher, translator, and example for all the other

15,000 Kogis in the tribe. We wanted to protect him and give him every possible advantage.

Any American that we asked for advice about taking Alfonso to the States gave thumbs down. It seemed that most people knew a story about the folly of taking a primitive Indian to the USA. One knew of an Indian who almost died because he wouldn't/couldn't eat American food. Others got sick and lonely and almost died; some even got pneumonia from the cold, and we were headed for Minnesota. One from the Philippines acculturated too much. He wanted a car and all the other amenities he saw among American young people. We were quite sure that none of the above would happen with Alfonso. He had been a part of our family now for almost three years. He loved our food. He got along great with our boys. We were pretty sure he wouldn't want a car. Others said it would take months, maybe years, to get all his papers in order to go to the United States. I, myself, was not even so sure that we should take him. My relatives in Minnesota really didn't feel comfortable with rubbing shoulders with people of other races. My dad didn't even believe that people of other races could be "saved" in this dispensation, and we would be living with my parents. When pressed he had admitted that in the mercy and goodness of God, some could be saved, but mainly their time would come in a future dispensation. I hated to lock horns with my dad over his dispensational beliefs, but Chad thought that seeing and knowing Alfonso would be a step in the right direction in dispelling his prejudices. I also had to admit that I would have to do a lot more cooking with Alfonso in the family. He had a huge appetite and ate twice as much as any of the rest of us. How would I fill him up without rice and plantains at every meal?

Our mission staff in Bogota, while not actually giving a thumbs down, informed Chad that no one on the Wycliffe staff would have time to help him get all Alfonso's papers in order. Chad would have to take the responsibility for that himself. Chad and I agreed together that we would lay the whole problem of whether or not Alfonso should go to the

USA before the Lord. We came to the conclusion that as long as the Lord opened doors for the necessary documents, starting with the birth certificate, we would go forward. If a door closed, we would send Alfonso back to Santiago.

So, as we left Santiago's farm and arrived at Carmelo, Alfonso was with us. While we were at Santiago's farm, Alfonso had gone to Don Diego to see his parents and get their permission to go with us to the USA. We had no idea at the time how blessed we were that Alfonso was not a part of a more formal village. He lived with Santiago, and probably the leadership in Don Diego had no idea that one of their young men was going to go to another country, much less to another continent. Alfonso's parents had consented to his going to Lomalinda with us because they wanted him to learn Spanish and to read and write. They probably thought the United States was some place just a little farther than Bogotá. As far as we know, not even the nine positive divinations required before Santiago and Wenceslau were allowed to go to Bogotá with Chad in October 1964 were required for Alfonso to go with us. The permissions would have to be given by the Colombian authorities and the United States embassy.

Chapter 30

Miracles of Paperwork

As we passed through Carmelo, the missionaries knew we were on our way to the USA, and they wondered why Alfonso was with us. When Chad told them he was going on our furlough with us, they were quite upset. One veteran missionary came over to the mule I was riding and gave me quite a talking to. We were making a big mistake, she told me. It would wreck our trip, which should be a time of rest and recuperation, and it would be a disaster for Alfonso. "Just look at him," she said as he ran along the muddy road with Russell, his bare feet splashing through the mud, his long, wild hair blowing in the wind. He wore the same spotted and stained filthy garment that he had worn all the way to Don Diego and back and who knows how many weeks before that. I had suggested to Chad that we should wait while Alfonso went to the river to bathe and change his clothes, but Chad was so happy that his pet Kogi had shown up in time to go with us, he thought it best to just bring him along as he was. "He can take a shower in Santa Marta," Chad told me.

"And if you SHOULD get him shaped up," continued the missionary with a doubtful look, "he would never fit back into his tribe again."

The missionaries in Santa Marta agreed to let Alfonso sleep in the mission house this time, instead of sending him off to a cheap hotel like they had Santiago and Wenceslau in 1963 (which turned out to be a house of prostitution). The condition was that we get him cleaned up first. He had a change of clothes along, and he knew how to bathe in a shower as that was what he had done in Lomalinda, but now he had been in the mountains, living an unfettered life for some three months. He was not at all sure he wanted to be told when and where he had to bathe. Chad had to use force to get him into the shower, and as soon as the offensive garment was thrown over the door of the shower stall, I saw to it that it didn't get put on again.

The next day, Chad and Alfonso went to Ciénaga to get the birth certificate. I was surprised to see Chad come barreling into the house around 11:00 a.m. "You have to come with me RIGHT NOW to Ciénaga," he insisted. Off I went. Once there, I was ushered into an office and asked to sign some papers. Everyone was extremely civil and friendly. We were told to come back in the afternoon for the birth certificate.

After we left the registrar's office, Chad told me what had happened. Chad stated Alfonso's birthdate as March 10, 1950. That made him 18 years old. Three years before, Santiago had told us he was 15, thus the age of 18 now. "I don't think he is that old," I demurred. "Well, he thinks he is 18, and we have to put down an age he will agree to," Chad insisted. Surely the Lord was directing in this, because had he been under 18, we would have had to go back to the tribe and bring both of his parents to sign a paper before a notary giving him permission to leave Colombia. One funny thing had happened: The registrar had asked Alfonso if his parents were married. Of course they were married, Alfonso replied. "By the padre (priest) in the iglesia (church)?" continued the registrar. "No, by the mama in the sierra," answered Alfonso.

All went well until the registrar told Chad that two people were needed to sign the document. "Can I sign?" asked Chad.

When the answer was affirmative, Chad signed. "Now, what about the other person?" asked the registrar.

"Can you sign?" asked Chad.

"No," was the reply, "I can't sign."

"Can the secretary sign?"

"No, she can't sign."

"Can my wife sign?" Chad was getting desperate.

"Yes, she can sign."

That accounted for the quick trip to Santa Marta to bring me to Ciénaga. Later we found out that we had signed that we were present at Alfonso's birth. (Many years later in a small town in Colombia, we found out that this rule was loosely interpreted. The registrars were anxious to get more of the undocumented children in rural Colombia registered. They would accept as witnesses anyone who seemed reliable and who would testify to the parentage of these children. In later years I personally served as a witness to register many country children in eastern Colombia.)

The next day with Alfonso's birth certificate in hand, we left for Bogotá. Now since he was 18 years old, Alfonso had to have a paper giving him an exemption from military service. Once the recruiting officer saw who he was, that paper was signed. Next came the Colombian passport. Chad was able to meet a special lawyer who helped with the paperwork to get Alfonso's passport. Upon Chad's signature that he would be sure to not let Alfonso go illegal and stay in the USA, a visa was given. In just two days, all the paperwork was complete, and Alfonso was all set to go to the USA.

Chapter 31

Furlough

Back at Lomalinda we received an enthusiastic welcome from Chaddy and Sharon. Lomalinda was abounding in excitement as a number of families and a few single people were preparing to go on furlough as soon as school was dismissed for the season. Furlough was what we called the year that missionaries spent in their home country after four or five years' service in a foreign land. For many of us, it was our first furlough, and we were busy consulting the more seasoned members of the branch who had joined us from Perú or México.

Some women were sewing new wardrobes to wear in the United States. Others said to throw everything away and start new once you got back to the stores in the USA. Chad was of this second opinion, but I felt that I needed to prepare at least a few new dresses for the girls and myself before we left Colombia. Some of the women had sewing patterns that they had brought with them, and the newcomers had some fairly recent styles. I ripped apart some of the girls' dresses and used them as patterns, cutting the new pieces a little larger.

One dress that I made for myself caused me a lot of grief. I started with a fairly recent pattern and a piece of perma-press material that one of the more recently arrived ladies gave me. It was a dark brown color, but I brightened it up by appliqueing a colorful design on the front. It was easy to make with just two main pieces, front and back. Since I was not very secure in my dressmaking skills, I took my dress, once the two pieces were sewn together, to all my seamstress friends on the base to ask their opinions. One took some darts at the waist; another one let them out again. One thought it was too long, another that it was too short. One pulled it in tight at the waist, and the last one took that adjustment out saying, "This is a baggy style." I learned that sewing a dress could not be a committee project. I wore that dress on the airplane, but I don't remember wearing it after that.

Since the mission took a certain amount of money out of each monthly support check to be used for our return trip to the USA, we had the money saved up to buy our tickets back to our homes. Chad and I only bought tickets to Miami. Chad's parents had retired and moved to Florida, and they would pick us up and take us to their new home on the gulf side of the peninsula for a short visit. Majel Meyer was still a good friend. She was living and working in Georgia. She wanted us to borrow her car to use during our furlough. We could take a Greyhound bus from Florida to Georgia where we would pick up the car.

The money that we had received from the sale of the cattle in North Dakota was almost gone. Our travel expenses from Florida to Minnesota would use up the rest of it as well as anything left over from the furlough fund. I didn't know what happened with missionaries on furlough. What did they do besides speaking in churches? Did anyone support them? This again was a new experience, and it made me very nervous. I was so thankful for a warm letter from my mother saying that they were making an additional bathroom in their basement and that our boys and Alfonso could sleep there. Chad and I with Gloria could have a bedroom upstairs, and Mother would figure out someplace where Sharon could sleep. They were really looking forward to having us back again.

Chad had applied and been accepted for a masters' program at the University of North Dakota. I agreed to take a few classes but opted out of the masters' program.

Our relationship with Chad's parents had always been rocky, and they really didn't want us to bring Alfonso to their new house. After much prayer and consideration, we decided that Chad and Russell would fly to Florida one week before the rest of us. They would have a week to spend with Chad's parents before the rest of us with Alfonso got there.

On the airplane to Miami, I sat next to Frances Jackson, a very dear single lady who was a support missionary at least ten years older than I. Frankie, as we called her, had spent some 25 years in Mexico before coming to help us in Colombia. She had been in charge of the group house in Bogota, and most recently ran the kitchen/dining room at Lomalinda. I knew she was from California, so I asked her what she was going to do when she got to Miami. I was expecting an answer like she was taking a connecting flight to California, or meeting friends in Miami.

"I'm going to find a restaurant and order a root beer," was her unexpected answer. Root beer was unknown in South America. We had Coca-Cola, Pepsi Cola, and a number of fruit flavors, such as orange and grape. We also had some flavors unknown in North America, like colombiana and manzana. Manzana was apple and colombiana was maybe related to cream soda. Our friend, Jim Walton, thought that colombiana tasted like the inside of a woman's purse smelled. We agreed it was an apt description, although we eventually learned to like it.

Chad and his father were waiting for us when we arrived in Miami. The trip seemed torturously long to Bonita Springs. We had to wind around the tip of Florida on old Highway 41. Interstate 75, Alligator Alley, was still a year or so in the future. We were duly impressed with Jean and Russell's new home. After a week or so, all seven of us climbed on a Greyhound bus for a small town near Macon, Georgia. Here a funny incident took place. Chad and Alfonso were busy with the luggage, so Chad gave me the tickets and sent me ahead to get on the bus with the children. I wasn't that great a Spanish speaker at that time, but for some reason, I could talk nothing but Spanish to the bus driver. When Chad finally boarded the bus, the driver handed Chad the mutilated tickets with the remark that Chad's wife had made him so nervous that he ripped the tickets in half. That seems very strange in light of the fact that now, over 45 years later, you can live in south Florida and get along just fine without knowing English.

Upon arrival at the house where Majel was living, we realized at once that the little car she was loaning us was not going to be big enough for us and all our suitcases. I volunteered to go on the bus with the girls and the biggest suitcases all the way to Minnesota. That left room in the car for Chad, Alfonso, the two boys, and the smaller suitcases. I decided I had better wash the accumulation of dirty clothes before we set out on the next phase of our journey. Majel directed me to the neighborhood Laundromat. A sign in the window said, "Whites Only."

That is strange, I thought, but perhaps the owners think that colored clothes will stain the insides of their automatic washing machines. I only had one white load, and after I got that going, I was looking around to see where I could wash my colored clothes. To my surprise, I saw other women loading washers with colored clothes. Following their example, I loaded all of my other clothes into the machines. When I got back to the house, I asked Majel what the sign meant. To my surprise, she told me that there was another Laundromat around the corner and down the alley for the black people. That was my only encounter with the segregation of the south.

The trip from Georgia to Minneapolis was quite an experience. I held three-year-old Gloria on my lap the entire trip. Bus travel was still very popular, and the buses were crowded. I had my first experience with Kentucky Fried Chicken when the bus made a stop in Kentucky. I thought it was a very nicely done local restaurant dedicated to a local hero, Colonel Sanders. Farther north we had our first experience with the golden arches at another bus stop. I was quite pleased with both eating experiences, and I was very surprised to find Kentucky Fried Chicken all the way up to Minnesota. Later, McDonald's became quite a fixture in our lives. Both restaurants had come into being while we were in Colombia. Previously White Castle hamburgers and A&W Root Beer Stand had been the places we went for an inexpensive treat.

We rode on the bus all night. Both girls slept, Gloria in my arms, and Sharon with her head on my shoulder. I was afraid to go to sleep for fear I would drop Gloria, so I made my eyes stay open all night. By the second day, this bus ride was getting tiresome. Finally we traveled through Wisconsin, and I almost cried with nostalgia to see Scandinavian-looking women with the short permed hair grey that was in style among my relatives and my mother's friends get on the bus. They looked so familiar; I realized I was almost home.

Truly the longest mile (or the longest 100 miles) was the last mile home. At last the bus arrived in the downtown Minneapolis station, and there through the window I could see Mother and Dad, a little older, a little greyer, anxiously scanning the passengers alighting from the bus. I sent Gloria out first. The grandparents had never seen her, but of course they recognized her at once from the pictures I had sent. As they enveloped her in hugs, Sharon came down the steps. She was only five, a kindergartener, when they had seen her last. Now she was a young lady of nine. Finally I got our sweaters and other items gathered and descended the stairs of the bus. What a wonderful reunion it was.

My parents saw at once how tired I was, and my mother started berating herself for not having sent us money to buy tickets to travel on an airplane. Chad and the boys arrived at almost the same time that we did, so it was a wonderful reunion back at 4440 Bryant Avenue South.

I felt like an alien who had arrived from another planet to a place where I had previously lived eons ago. It seemed so strange that Bryant Avenue should still exist, as well as the house where I grew up, and the schools that I attended. It was all there, so different from Santiago's farm, the village of Mamarongo, Lomalinda, and even the city of Bogotá. The streets were clean, the automobiles drove in an orderly fashion, and English was spoken on all sides.

There were changes though. Interstate 35W had cut through the city only a few blocks from my parents' house, taking out an entire block of familiar houses. My mother warned me that there had been other changes as well. We could no longer allow the children to go the five or six blocks down to Lake Harriet without an adult, she told me. People had been attacked on the footpaths through the park and around the lake. Doors on houses and cars had to be kept locked. But some changes were good. Within a few days she took me to a huge store, the Holiday Store. This was a precursor to the Kmarts and Walmarts that would come later. "You can get anything you want here." she told me, "If you can't find it here, you don't need it."

Dorothe and her family arrived before long, and soon we were all happily interacting together. Alfonso too was included as one of the family. If anyone was still bothered by racial prejudice, they kept it to themselves. Dorothe had a new little son, just three months older than Gloria. Dorothe took the girls and me out and bought us each a new dress so we would have something nice for speaking engagements. But there was a cloud on the joyful family reunion. Mother and Dorothe took me aside and told me the sad story of Darrell's death some seven months before.

Chapter 32

Darrell's Story

No baby was ever awaited with more joy and anticipation than was our little brother Darrell. Our mother was never very strong and probably had suffered physical damage from a severe case of scarlet fever in her childhood. She always had to "save some strength to get dinner" as she put it as she rested in the afternoons. Her pregnancies and birthing experiences had been horrendous to hear her tell it. Now in 1936, at 40 years of age, she was less than thrilled to find out that she was pregnant again. In her fear and dismay, she was comforted by a verse in the first book of Timothy that spoke of women being saved in childbearing. There are a number of theological interpretations of 1 Timothy 2:15, but to my mother the "being saved" meant being saved from the pain and anguish that she had experienced bringing her other children into the world.

She decided to "take this baby by faith." Soon even I at seven years of age could tell that something had happened to our fragile mother. She filled our basement "vegetable room" with home-canned fruits, vegetables, pickles, jams and jellies. Then she started redecorating the house, even painting, although the smell of paint had always made her feel sick both before and even after this pregnancy. This surge of well-being continued all the way up to the spring morning, the day before Easter, 1937, when she went to the hospital for the arrival of the baby.

Of course no one knew the sex of the baby, but along with everything else, Mother was taking it by faith that the baby would be a boy. She planned to call him Richard after my father. The labor took its course, and in due time Mother was taken into the delivery room. My parents had hand-picked a reliable Christian doctor in whom they both had utter confidence. The doctor explained to Mother that he would not be able to give her any anesthetic to which she agreed.

I can't imagine a wise doctor doing such a thing, but of course this was over seventy years ago when perhaps patient psychology was not a part of the doctor's training. As the delivery neared the end, according to my mother, the doctor remarked to the nurses and an intern who was in attendance, "I don't see how this baby can be born. He has such a big head."

Upon hearing this, as can be imagined, my mother panicked. Then the inner voice of the Lord penetrated her heart and mind, "I thought you were taking this baby by faith."

"Yes, I will trust you, Lord," was my mother's heart response.

As my mother told the story many times in my hearing, she was caught up into heaven where she saw a shimmering light and experienced things too wonderful for words. When she came back to consciousness of the delivery room again, the baby boy had been born, and she was praising the Lord.

Later, the intern came to her hospital room to ask her about what had happened in the delivery room. He said that he had heard many women cursing God in the delivery room, but he had never heard one praising Him as Mother had done.

Mother was a great "soul winner" and she thought that when she left the hospital and told people about her experience in the delivery room, everyone would believe and turn to the Lord. However, she could not coherently explain the experience, and usually just ended up crying and saying that she had been caught up into heaven. Most people believed that she had been anesthetized.

Dad would not allow the baby to be named for him, so eventually they decided to name him Darrell. With the birth of Darrell, my parents felt that their family was complete – two girls and a boy. They felt that he was a very special little boy. As he grew up everything he did was considered smart and cute. He got by with things that Dorothe and I would never have been allowed to do. He received much praise when he went to school – his first-grade teacher saying that she hoped she had a little boy just like him. In Sunday school as well, he had the approval of all of his teachers. Several were just sure that he would be a preacher someday. Of course Mother beamed at all the good comments about her son.

It is hard to say when the change began. As his teenage years progressed, Darrell lost all interest in school and church. His love became the outdoors – hunting and fishing. He loved to hang around the local filling station with a gang of like-minded youths. He started to drink beer and smoke cigarettes, activities that our parents and their friends condemned. He entered into an early and probably unwise marriage and fathered three sons. It was a blessing that this was all before the days of drugs, and I never heard of him being a drinker of hard liquor; however, the beer was enough. He was often drunk, and my parents – two old grey-haired rescue mission workers – had to roam the streets of lower Minneapolis, looking for their son, whom I believe they found drunk in the gutters more than a few times. I was away from home during much of this time with very little contact with Darrell; however,

Chad and I joined my parents down on our knees in our family home to pray for Darrell on several occasions and lifted Darrell up to God in prayer regularly in our daily prayer times. Dorothe was also away from home during much of this time, but being closer in age to Darrell and having had more in common with him as they were growing up, she was very, very concerned for his recovery.

Because of DUIs, Darrell rarely had a valid driver's license. Dad got him a job at the US Post Office as a mail carrier, and even after Dad retired, he often had to pick

him up in the mornings and take him to work. I loved Darrell very much, but by the time we left for Colombia, we had very little contact with him. I hoped that perhaps someday we could bring him to Lomalinda for a visit, and he could see another side of life and Christianity from that which he had experienced in Minnesota. That dream was destroyed by the happenings of November 3, 1967. Now that I was back home again, I would get a chance to learn from Mother and Dorothe what really transpired that day and in the weeks that followed.

Chapter 33

Something Special

As Chad and I enjoyed Chad's 40th birthday party in Lomalinda, little did we know what was happening meanwhile back at our family home in Minneapolis. Now seven months later, Mother and Dorothe had the opportunity to tell me what had happened from their viewpoint.

Dorothe and her husband, Ralph, had taken a Campus Crusade course in personal evangelism that autumn and had been very blessed by what they had learned. Several times they remarked to one another that it would be so wonderful if someone from this class could go to talk with Darrell. They knew that as family members they would not be given the same hearing that common courtesy would accord to a stranger. As the class drew to an end, the members were sent out two by two to fulfill the assignment of visiting six homes to present the plan of salvation to whoever was there. Dorothe and Ralph prayed that someone from that class or a similar class would call on Darrell.

On November 3, Darrell joined a party of men for a duck hunting trip up into northern Minnesota. Darrell, I was told, had injured his knee. It was stiff, and he was contemplating surgery in the near future. He had dressed in very heavy clothing against the chill of November. It was often 20 degrees colder in northern Minnesota than in Minneapolis, some 200 miles to the south. As the men cruised the icy water, looking for ducks, whatever boat or canoe they were in overturned. The paddles or oars were lost, but the men were able to right the craft, and all of them but Darrell were able to climb into the boat. Because of Darrell's bad knee and heavy water-soaked clothing, Darrell was not able to get in, so he hung onto the boat while the others paddled to shore using their hands. When they got to the shore, they found that Darrell had died of hypothermia from the cold water. He was still clinging to the boat.

Of course this news was a terrible shock to everyone that knew our family. Our parents were devastated. Dorothe and Mother told me that Dad had never fully recovered from the shock. It had been a great grief to him that Chad and I had gone to Colombia and taken Russell, Chaddy, and Sharon, his grandchildren to whom he was very attached, and then the loss of his only son added another crippling blow. The news of Darrell's death was carried by the Minneapolis newspaper, and calls of condolence started pouring in. Two of these calls from strangers were especially welcome to my mother.

One of these calls came from a man who had attended a Campus Crusade class in personal evangelism. He and his companion had completed their assignment of visiting six homes. They were on their way back to their car when they passed the house where Darrell lived. Something about that house beckoned to them. As Mother described it, she said that the house "lit up." The man said that they just had to visit that house.

Inside they found Darrell on the front porch, while his wife was in the kitchen preparing the evening meal. One man visited with Darrell, while the other one went to the kitchen to talk with the wife. Campus Crusade uses a rather canned approach—either the Four Spiritual Laws or something similar. Chad teaches that it would be better to have the Holy

Spirit lead in a message especially designed for each person. However, as this man started in with his message, Darrell interrupted him. "I know all that," Darrell told him. "I used to be a Christian when I was a boy, but I got away from it."

"Wouldn't you like to come back to the Lord?" The man asked him. Darrell said that he would, and the two prayed together. When the man saw the notice in the newspaper of Darrell's accidental death, he knew that he had to call my parents to tell what had happened. Darrell had not told his parents about this happening, but later Mother recalled that in two telephone conversations with her, Darrell had tried to tell her about his return to the Lord, but somehow he stopped short of actually saying the words.

Then came another welcome telephone call. Every morning, Darrell as a mail carrier had to "put up his mail." This involved working at a table at the branch post office, organizing his mail for delivery. Other mail carriers worked at tables on each side of him. The two men who worked on either side of Darrell told Mother that there had been a big change in Darrell the last two weeks of his life. His language had cleaned up, and he told them that he had returned to the Lord.

These calls made Mother so happy that she was still rejoicing seven months later to think that the son whom she had had to go looking for in the gutters and saloons of lower Minneapolis was now safely in heaven.

Many people from many different walks of life attended the funeral. Darrell was buried in a family lot in beautiful Lakewood Cemetery, a huge cemetery with rolling green hills, right by Lake Harriet and up against a large wooded area known as the Bird Refuge. As a boy, Darrell spent most of his waking hours in the summer and after school on the shores of Lake Harriet or in the Bird Refuge. He was laid to rest next to his paternal grandparents and an uncle who died as a teenager. Later my parents would be buried in the same plot. He was 30 years old.

Mother said that during the graveside ceremony, a beautiful Chinese pheasant, a brilliantly-colored game bird (a species that was imported into South Dakota and Minnesota long before my lifetime) that Darrell loved to hunt, walked through the cemetery among the mourners, and overhead flew a large, green-headed mallard duck. To my mother, these were signs from the Lord that her son was in heaven. Mother again saw the same shimmering light that she had seen at Darrell's birth.

The pastor said that as he brought the closing words at the graveside, he could tell who was a Christian and who was not. All the faces of the Christians shone with a heavenly light.

Dorothe remembered that the morning of Darrell's death she had prayed in her morning prayer time, "Lord, do something special for Darrell today."

Chapter 34

Respected but Broke

After a wonderful week, we Stendals crowded into Majel's little car, leaving most of our suitcases in Minneapolis, and headed north for the University of North Dakota. It was sad to leave our family after such a short visit, but we knew we would be back.

Our reception at the university was quite different from our lowly entrance in 1962. This time we were coming back as third-year students, having spent four years actually doing that for which the first- and second-year students were now training. Even the instructors accorded us a certain amount of respect. Colombia was rated as one of the more difficult of the Wycliffe fields of service, and what's more, we even had an exotic-looking Kogi Indian along with us as friend and language resource person. We were under the direct supervision and instruction of Dr. Richard Pitman, the director of the North Dakota branch of the Summer Institute of Linguistics.

In spite of a certain amount of opposition from Dr. Pitman, I succeeded in taking a very light load. At this point, I had the same number of linguistics credits on the graduate level as Chad did, but outside of the third-year linguistics course, taught by Dr. Pitman himself for which he insisted that I register, I don't remember that I took anything else that session. In order to earn a master's degree, I would have to write a thesis and accumulate credits for a minor, and since I knew I was not going to do that (I would have to devote whatever time I had to acting as Chad's secretary for his thesis and anthropology studies for his minor) I could see no point in taking more credits myself. I told him that I had come from a very strenuous four years in Colombia, and that I needed a rest, but he pooh-poohed that idea. He finally gave in, saying that since I would have all my linguistics credits lined up, I could finish my master's degree on my next furlough when we would be farther along with our linguistics studies and have more options for writing a thesis.

I really did not feel well. I had been pushing myself physically ever since I had started having the malaria attacks. I would just start to feel more energetic when suddenly I would be struck down by another attack. Much of the time on this furlough I felt as though I were looking out at the world through a haze, or perhaps through smoked glasses. It was not my eyes, but rather something to do with my head or my perception. I didn't feel "quite there" much of the time.

Our whole family underwent physical examinations while we were at the Summer Institute of Linguistics. This was a Wycliffe requirement to make sure we were all fit to return to Colombia for another term. We didn't say much to the doctor. We certainly didn't want to make a lot of complaints and give him the impression that we were too sick to go back.

My other big worry was the money. At the university we had many expenses. In addition to the tuition, we had to pay board and room for seven people and child care for four children. All the three older children were with the school-age kids, and in addition to swimming lessons, many interesting activities were planned for them. They were soon happy with friends old and new. Gloria, who was now turning four, was all right in the nursery, but in the middle of the summer she came down with mumps and was excluded. I brought her meals to the room that she shared with us, and she was happy all day, nibbling her food and playing with the few games and toys I was able to find for her. Actually, she ended up cleaning her plate and eating more food with the mumps than she did when she was well and limited to mealtimes. We made a payment on our bill at the finance office, and that left us with very little money in Chad's pocket.

In one sense, we were heroes among the staff and students. We had actually gone to Colombia, which was considered to be one of the difficult and delicate fields of service, and contacted and entered a hitherto unreached tribe. Here was Alfonso with his traditional white clothes and long, wild hair as living proof of our accomplishment. Chad confided our financial embarrassment to the financial officers of SIL and was told that as speaking opportunities arose in the community, they would be directed his way.

THE STENDALS
Russell, Gloria, Chad, Chaddy, Pat, Alfonso, Sharon

SERVES AS INTERPRETER

Boy Ignores Death Threats

THE MINNEAPOLIS STAR

News of the Churches

Sat., Nov. 30, 1968   THE MINNEAPOLIS STAR   ★   11A

An 18-year-old boy from the Kogi Indian tribe in the remote mountains of Colombia is helping a Minneapolis missionary couple reduce his language to writing, despite death threats from his village chiefs.

The boy, known only as Alfonso, has lived with Mr. and Mrs. Chad Stendal for 3½ years. His parents left him with the Stendals when they were in Colombia because they wanted him to learn how to speak and read Spanish.

He not only has done this but he has learned to read his own language after assisting the Stendals in developing an alphabet, grammar and primers in it.

The Stendals have begun a translation of the Kogi Old Testament into Kogi and hope eventually to also translate the New Testament into it, as well as materials on health, farming and other subjects.

When he is serving as their language informant, the Stendals pay Alfonso a small wage. He used it to buy a bicycle, which was stolen while the Stendals have been living at 4440 Bryant Av. S. Police later recovered it. Alfonso also has weaved himself two suits while he has been in Minneapolis.

The Stendals said that to their knowledge no Kogi Indian man has ever cut his hair or exchanged his handwoven tribal dress for the shirt and pants of his Colombia neighbors.

They said it is a crime, punishable by poisoning, for Kogis to give information to outsiders on their language and culture.

Disregarding this taboo, a small group of Kogis living in an isolated valley accepted the Stendals. The group included Alfonso, who has been threatened by the chiefs of his own village.

News of the Stendals' medical work among the small group spread to Mamarongo where a seriously ill chief overcame his suspicions enough to call for their help.

When his health was restored, the Stendals received permission to visit the village, although other villagers objected.

The Stendal son, Chaddy, then 10, and Alfonso went alone into Mamaron-go on the first flight of the small plane that eventually brought the rest of the Stendals and their cargo there. Because of plane difficulties, the later flights were delayed and the two boys were alone in the village with the Kogis for the first four days.

"By the time we got there, our son had already worked his way into the hearts of the people of Mamarongo," the Stendals said.

The Stendals who came to the states last June, will return to Colombia in February with their four children and Alfonso. They hope that Alfonso will eventually be able to bring the message of Christ to his own people.

The Stendals work under auspices of the Wycliffe Bible Translators and are partially supported by the Bethany Fellowship of Bloomington, to which they belong.

ALFONSO WITH HIS ONCE-STOLEN BICYCLE
He bought it with money earned in translation work

Chapter 35

A Friendly Church

By the time the first weekend rolled around, we were starting to feel at home in our cozy rooms in the university dormitory. Saturday night Chad and I entered into a discussion about the churches in Grand Forks and attempted to come to an agreement as to where we should attend services on the following morning. Being very much a people person, I wanted to find just one friendly congregation and faithfully attend that same church all summer. In our previous summers at Grand Forks, we had sampled a lot of different churches, but we had never really made friends anywhere. After talking with several lady friends at Lomalinda, I was convinced that the friendly church in the area was the Lutheran Brethren Church, one that we had not yet visited. Chad wanted to attend a small Pentecostal church in the area where he remembered having enjoyed the music. Usually we did things Chad's way, but on this occasion I held very firmly to my opinion and won the argument. I was really anxious to make some friends in the community.

The next morning, we all crammed ourselves into the little car and started off for the new church. Before we had gone very far, Chad noticed that a tire was low, and pulled into a service station. While he was trying to put air in the tire, the radiator started boiling. By the time Chad had changed the tire and put water into the radiator, we realized that the church service was over, and it was time for dinner at the university dormitory. After paying the service station attendant for fixing the tire, there was now only small change in Chad's pocket, and I didn't have a cent. We really wondered how we would get through the month of June; however, there was still some gas in the little grey Lark.

The next Sunday, Chad announced that since we had spent the entire time of the Sunday service in the service station, this time HE would pick the church. The Lutheran church may have been a fine church, but obviously God didn't want us in that church; this was Chad's reasoning. We all piled into the little car again, and this time we went to the little Pentecostal church on the edge of town. We arrived at the church early, in time for Sunday School. The pastor had changed during the last four years, and he stood in the doorway greeting the children and adults as we entered the church. Surely he had watched as our crew ambled up the front sidewalk, Chad in his outdated suit and tie, and me with the four children in tow, plus Alfonso in his typical Kogi outfit.

"You folks missionaries?" he questioned as he greeted Chad with a handshake.

"How did you ever guess?" was Chad's reply.

"Got any slides of your ministry?" continued Pastor Riveness.

"Only a few thousand well-chosen slides," answered Chad with a grin.

"Can you come back to church tonight and show us a few?"

No one except my mother had shown any interest in our slides up to now, so this was really a great invitation. Of course we agreed to return. By this time the children, Alfonso, and I were all seated in the big assembly room of the Sunday school. After an opening song or two, a big announcement was made about the opening of the summer camp of the denomination a few weeks away. The children were all encouraged to register for camp as soon as possible.

As soon as Sunday school ended, the children ran to Chad and me begging to go to camp. That sounded like a good idea, but where was the money to come from? We looked for the friendly pastor and laid the matter before him. He offered to go ahead and register Russell, Chaddy, and Sharon, and said that later we could pay him a much-discounted fee for their week at camp. That was great, but after the morning service we were accosted by Alfonso. He wanted to go to camp too. The pastor consulted with his elders and came back to say that the camp would be happy to receive Alfonso for the week as a guest of camp.

My mother had loaned us her slide projector, so we spent the afternoon choosing a tray of colored slides to present at the church. The service that evening went very well. After a few hymns, a man played an organ solo, and then we were on to show the slides. Our presentation seemed to be well received, and then following the offering and sermon, the meeting was dismissed. The people were friendly, coming up to shake hands with us and commenting on how much they liked the slides and how happy they were that Alfonso and the children were going to camp. Before we left the building, the pastor came up and placed in Chad's hands a manila envelope containing the entire offering of the evening. This was a tremendous miracle and blessing for us poor missionaries who had only a few cents to our name at this point. Monday after my class, I went out and bought the items of clothing needed by the children in order to go to the camp and also put gas in the car.

The next evening Chad was called to the telephone. It was Pastor Dave Riveness. He was calling to tell Chad some exciting news. Dave Riveness was the chairman in charge of the summer camp this year. He had invited several area pastors to be the camp speaker, but each one turned him down because of other commitments. He finally thought of his old friend, Arthur Sather, a pastor out in the Seattle, Washington area. Pastor Art consented to be the camp speaker. Pastor Dave was calling to tell us about a call that he had just received from

Pastor Art. Art asked him to call the University of North Dakota and try to reach a man named Chad Stendal. "That won't be hard," answered Dave. "He spoke in my church last night."

"Also," continued Dave, "You are going to have one of those Kogi Indians that you are always talking about under your ministry at camp next week."

"And that's not all," continued Dave addressing Chad. "Did you notice that organ in the church last night?" Chad replied that he had.

"Well, I had it brought in on consignment, and I was planning to use the offering for the down payment. However, just as I was receiving the offering, the Lord spoke to my heart, 'Give the entire offering to the Stendals.' I was surprised, but I did as the Lord said."

"Monday morning I received a phone call from a well-to-do church member. 'I kind of like that organ that you had in the church last night. How much does it cost?' he said. I named the figure, and he surprised me by saying, 'I am putting a check for that amount in the mail this morning.'"

Pastor Dave's voice was full of praise and joy for the way his obedience had paved the way for this great blessing for the church. We too were thrilled to hear the way that the Lord was providing for our needs as well as blessing the church.

"Pastor Art is arriving in Grand Rapids on Wednesday," continued our new friend, Pastor Dave. "He wants me to set up an appointment with you folks. He wants to meet you before he goes out to camp."

Although our schedule was quite heavy, we managed to find an evening hour in which to spend some time with Pastor Art at the university. This was the man whose brother-in-law had run into Chad with Alfonso and Santiago at Lomalinda. Art and his wife Verdie had been praying for years for a tribe of small people in the mountains of northern Colombia. They called them "pygmies" and had endured a lot of ridicule from people who knowingly stated that "the pygmies are in Africa." This had been the opinion of the brother-in-law until he ran into Chad with the Kogis. Santiago measured 4 ft. 6 in. in height, and at that time Alfonso was even shorter.

Pastor Art invited us to the closing meeting at the campground on the Sunday afternoon after camp. Chad agreed to attend with only one reservation. He had been assigned two speaking assignments on that Sunday morning, and we didn't know if time and distance would make it possible to be at the camp meeting. However, the Lord had it all in hand. The assigned meetings were at 10:00 and 11:00 a.m. at two small Presbyterian churches, normally served by one pastor who was going to be on vacation that week. When we looked at the map, we discovered these churches to be in the two towns nearest to the campground. There was even time for a quick lunch at a diner after the services.

The afternoon meeting was a great event. First Pastor Art Sather spoke, telling how he and his wife had received a supernatural message from God to pray for a small people with a strange language and customs, living in the mountains of northern Colombia, and then how he learned of us through his brother-in-law who served as a short-term pilot in Colombia. The focus of the prayer was to be that the Word of God be sent to them. Then Chad, a member of the Wycliffe Bible Translators, told how he had been led to the Kogi tribe from his job as a civil engineer with the St. Paul District U.S. Army Corp of Engineers. The meeting went so well that Pastor Art invited Chad and Alfonso to visit the churches on the West Coast as soon as Chad's studies for his master's degree in linguistics were completed.

We arrived back in Grand Rapids in time for Chad to speak at the evening service in a local Baptist church, also arranged by his friend in the office of the Summer Institute of Linguistics. The honorariums for these meetings replenished our financial supply, and we were able to meet our obligations at the financial office.

Chapter 36

The Menace of the Snow

The summer went quickly, and soon it was time to leave Grand Forks. I still was not feeling very well, but nothing much was demanded of me, so I got along all right. I was rather sad that we really had not made any progress on our analysis of the Kogi sound system. I had Alfonso say some of our most phonetically complicated and confusing words to some of the phonetics instructors. They shook their heads and pronounced them to be interesting, but they really didn't give any opinions that would help in the analysis. However, Dr. Pitman and Chad had shaped up an analysis of the discourse structure of the Kogi language to be written up as Chad's thesis.

Back in Minneapolis at my parents' house, we organized ourselves to live together for the winter months. Sharon and Chaddy started fifth and sixth grades at Clara Barton Grade School, the school that I had attended just two blocks from home. Russell enrolled in Ramsey Junior High, about a mile away. Chad registered at the University of Minnesota as a graduate student. He needed a minor in something that would be compatible with an MA degree in linguistics. He chose anthropology and had to take every course that was offered at the graduate level that quarter in order to get enough credits for the minor. It was rather a weird switch – an undergraduate degree in civil engineering, and an MA in linguistics with a minor in anthropology. He had none of the prerequisites for the graduate-level courses, but he managed to get the permission of the professors to take the courses. One of the courses was evolution, and he was able to write a term paper disproving evolution the way it was taught in the course. He received an A for his scholarship.

We purchased a Smith-Corona electric typewriter, the cusp of the wave as far as the technology of 1968 was concerned. Dorothe arranged for us to speak at Missionary Fellowship, a monthly meeting of generous business people, many of them Amway dealers, who donated to a specific missionary need each month. They wanted their donations to go to something extra that the missionary would not otherwise have, but which would facilitate their ministry. The electric typewriter was exactly the type of item they wanted to purchase for a missionary. This was a giant step above the old office Remington we had been using and even the little Olivetti portable that we had purchased to use in the tribe. The touch was so soft; I couldn't even believe I was typing. However, copies still had to be made with carbon paper, and errors laboriously erased with a special little eraser like a pencil with a brush on the other end. Soon we discovered a new item – correction tape. You could tear off a small piece and insert it over the letters to be corrected. It wrote white over the faulty letters. Then you removed the little pieces of tape through all the copies, and you could strike the correct characters. What a marvel this was, I thought. Using this marvelous machine, I was able to type the term papers required for Chad's anthropology courses as well as the thesis to be submitted to the University of North Dakota.

While Chad was attending classes at the University of Minnesota, Alfonso undertook the task of weaving himself some winter clothes. He had brought the wooden parts that he needed for the loom from the tribal area, and Chad bought him some wonderful soft, warm white yarn – lots of it. He set up the loom in Mother's living room to the wonder and amazement of all of her friends and proceeded to weave two complete outfits of warm Kogi men's clothes. When the snow started to fall, he was ready.

Mother and I shopped for the items we would need to take back to Colombia. I was obsessed with perma-press. I got some sheets and dresses for the girls and me. I especially made sure that I had plenty of dress pants for Chad and the boys as well as Sunday shirts. The electric generator at Lomalinda was not strong enough to permit us to iron, and now I wouldn't have to worry about wrinkled clothes. What a marvelous invention, I thought.

We received quite a few speaking engagements in the Minneapolis area where we showed our slides and told about Colombia. Everyone wanted to see Alfonso. He was rather shy and would only get up and say a few words in his language if Chad absolutely made him. Sometimes the children would sing a Spanish song for the people, and once in a while Chad would make Russell give a little word of greeting. All of this participation from the children was rather like pulling teeth, but the people really enjoyed it. Mother went to all of our meetings with us. She and I attended quite a few women's meetings, and this was the most fun of all as I could really share my heart with the missionary-minded women. Our

slides were very special as the Kogis with their distinctive appearance, white clothes, and red-and-white-striped carrying bags against the green tropical foliage looked great on Kodachrome film.

The day of the first snowfall was quite traumatic for poor Alfonso. He had been taught by Santiago as they looked at the snowcapped peaks of the Sierra Nevada de Santa Marta that the snow was made by the spirits of the dead. The precipitation during the rainy season accumulated as snow on the high mountain peaks. In the dry season, it slowly melted, running down the steep slopes as raging rivers and forming icy mountain lakes with special religious significance for the Kogi. We later found out that water was very sacred to the Kogi as their deity had arisen out of the water. It was the only thing more powerful and sacred than their Ancient Mother. Chad had explained a lot about weather, climate, etc. to Alfonso, but still, he seemed to be upset one Saturday morning when large wet snowdrops started falling from the sky. He walked from window to window looking pensive, and perhaps more than a little bit scared. As he saw the excitement among our children as they donned their warm jackets and mittens and headed out to play in the soft, wet snow, he relaxed a bit. I'm not sure if he joined them outside or not.

The next day, which was Sunday, we were scheduled to speak at the Sunday school hour for a large mainline church in south Minneapolis. Perhaps the sudden change in temperature and heavy snowfall had caught us all unaware. By the time we had the children, Alfonso, and ourselves all clad in boots, scarfs, mittens, etc. we were a little bit late in getting to the service. We found the parish hall full of adults and children sitting in silence as we set up the projector. To our horror, we found that as we started the slide showing, the lens of the projector was frosted over. The audience sat in silence, the room was cold, and the projector was very slow to warm up. Towards the end of the hour, we were able to show some of the slides. I imagine that Chad got up and spoke while we were waiting for the frost on the lens to thaw. I only remember being very embarrassed and uneasy. However, my shame was mild compared with what was to come.

When we finally got everything packed up again and got to the front door, a terrible sight met our eyes. The parishioners coming to church for their morning service were being snowballed as they walked up the curved sidewalk to their sanctuary. Our two boys and Alfonso were happily bombarding them with the wet snow. Snowballing is absolutely prohibited in Minneapolis on public property, school playgrounds, etc. It is considered very dangerous as serious injuries have been caused by an embedded rock or piece of ice in the snowball. As a Minneapolis teacher, every year I taught my class the evils of throwing snowballs. Here were my boys plus Alfonso throwing snowballs at dignified adults who were trying to get to their worship service on this cold snowy morning. Undoubtedly it was our fault for not anticipating this problem. At any rate, Alfonso seemed to have overcome his fear of the snow.

Chapter 37

Seattle, Back and Forth

Soon after we arrived in Minneapolis, we were invited to speak and show our slides at a church not far away from the neighborhood where my parents lived. Dorothe and her family also joined us for this evening service. Dorothe's family and my parents left at the close of the service, and Chad and I lingered to pack up the equipment and visit with the people of the church. Finally we too left. Imagine our surprise and consternation to find that Sharon had not returned to my parents' house with the others. Where was Sharon? We dialed the church, but no one answered. Chad was just getting ready to return to the church when a car drove up, and out hopped Sharon. Soon we heard her story.

Everyone had left the church, and she didn't know what to do. One family was still there to turn off the lights and close up the church. She approached one of the adults and explained that she had been left behind. They asked where she lived, but all she could say was that she lived with her grandparents. She didn't know the address or telephone number. Finally one of the adults asked her if she went to school, and upon receiving a positive answer, asked her the name of the school. She knew it was Clara Barton Elementary, so her good Samaritans drove her to the school. Then she indicated to them the route that she walked to return to her grandparents' house. After that, you can be sure that we taught the children their new address and telephone number.

After an enjoyable Christmas spent with my parents and Dorothe and her family, Chad and I with Gloria and Alfonso headed out to the West Coast to accept the invitation of Art Sather. Mother kindly consented to care for our three school-aged children in our absence. Chad was able to buy two clergy tickets for the two of us at half price. Gloria at 4 years old traveled free of charge. We only had to purchase one ticket for Alfonso at the full fare.

We stopped in Idaho where some friends from Minnesota were now living. Soon after our arrival, I succumbed to a flu that was going around followed by another attack of malaria. The guest room was in the basement where the children also played, and I was surprised to overhear Alfonso talking English with the boys of the household. He had never said anything in English to any of us.

Finally we had to move on to arrive in Seattle in time for the services that Pastor Art had scheduled for us. I was still very weak, so Chad decided to reserve a room for Gloria and me in the sleeping car. One evening about nine, we boarded the train. I headed for the sleeping bunk indicated by the number on my ticket but was stopped by the porter. "Don't go in there," he shouted bruskly. "There is a woman with three children trying to sleep in there." Gloria and I were ushered to a club car, and in about two hours, the porter came to escort us to our sleeping compartment. I don't know how the woman with three children managed, but I could not find any spot to accommodate Gloria except on top of my stomach. All went well for a while, but sometime in the wee hours, I got the urge to go to the bathroom. Since the toilet was beneath the bed, I had to stand the still -sleeping Gloria in the corridor while I folded up the bunk to access the toilet. I don't think I slept much, but when daylight came, I could see that the snow had been replaced by green grass. That was a welcome relief to all of us, but especially Alfonso and me.

We spent two or three wonderful weeks with Art and his wife Verdie. They had an event scheduled for us just about every night. Art usually accompanied us to tell his side of the story about the small people up in the mountains with the strange language, then Chad told his side, and I showed our slides. There are missionaries and pastors all over North America who have told me they received their call to full -time Christian service when Chad and Alfonso were in these meetings in the greater Seattle area.

Our train trip back to Minneapolis was more eventful. Alfonso succumbed to the flu and spent a miserable trip wrapped in a fuzzy blue blanket that Chad purchased somewhere when Alfonso went into chills and fever. We gave up the idea of the sleeping car, but the coach seats reclined and were fairly comfortable. Somewhere in the Dakotas, the train became snowbound. The snow was falling faster than the railroad snowplows could clear the tracks. Food ran out, and the dining car was closed, although snacks were still available. We were all tired and hungry; Alfonso was sick;

and Gloria was fussy. We were very happy when our train finally pulled into the Minneapolis station, and we were met by Dad. After a few weeks at 4440 Bryant Avenue, Chad and Alfonso headed back to Seattle, this time taking Russell with them; Art had more meetings scheduled for them. Art had asked about our support, and Chad had told him a minimal figure with which he thought we could manage.

Chapter 38

Colombia Again

After Chad and Russell arrived back in Minneapolis, happy that three churches in the Seattle area had pledged support to bring our income to the figure that Chad had mentioned, we decided to cut our year's furlough short and get back to Colombia so that our children could finish the school year at Lomalinda. Russell was due to graduate from eighth grade with his schoolmates. Our barrels were shipped, and our duffle bags and suitcases were packed. Once again we were faced with the lack of space in Majel Meyer's little grey Lark. We decided to buy thirteen-year-old Russell an airplane ticket to Florida to spend a few weeks with Chad's parents. Dorothe's family was driving to Alabama, so Sharon could ride with them and enjoy the friendship with her cousins for a few weeks more.

Chad and I with Alfonso, Chaddy, and Gloria headed south to Macon, Georgia to spend a few days with Majel Myer. Mother and Dad were left grieving for their grandchildren again, but Mother was also exhausted from the care of the children and all of us as we spent our time speaking, visiting, and packing. She and Dad went to stay for a while with her sister, so that Mother could rest up from her ordeal, both physical and emotional. I realized that staying with my parents had put too much strain on Mother. She had never been strong, and she was now in her seventies. I

vowed to find a different place to stay on our next furlough. Thankfully, she soon recovered.

Leaving Macon, we were somehow able to coordinate picking up nine-year-old Sharon in a bus station in South Georgia (not easy in those days before cell phones). We crowded her into the little car and continued south. After a week with Chad's parents, we were on our way to Miami and Colombia. Majel reclaimed her car in Miami, and off we went on a jet, taking much less time than the 6 hours on the 4 engine prop plane in 1964. What would we find on our return to Mamarongo? Were the Kogis in the area expecting us?

We arrived back in Lomalinda sometime at the end of April as I remember it. Our children soon joined their classes and seemingly had not suffered too much for missing several weeks of school, Russell more than the others. He was 13 and had grown immensely while we were in the USA. His voice had changed, and he was almost at his full height. I had noticed how fast he was growing while we were in Minneapolis, and I bought long dress pants in my beloved perma-press material in quite a few sizes longer than his present size. I also bought shoes for him to grow into several sizes larger in anticipation of his needs. Of course Chaddy, who was still quite short for his age, would be expected to grow into Russell's pants and clothes when Russell outgrew them as had always been the case. Our barrels had arrived from Minneapolis, and they were carefully unpacked, and the items for future use were repacked, and the barrels were stored in the long thin room in the center of the house that I had especially designed for that purpose. There was exactly room for the barrels in a long row with space enough to walk alongside and pack or unpack.

Finally in early June, school was out. All that was left was the closing program, including Russell's graduation from eighth grade. Each student in the graduating class was to give a short speech or sing an original song in honor of the occasion. We noticed that Russell had outgrown most of his classmates, but we were surprised by his behavior when his presentation was announced.

He was still quite timid about speaking before an audience, so he had decided to sing a song that he had composed, accompanying himself on a guitar. A wooden bench had been placed inconspicuously behind the pulpit so that the shorter members of the class could be seen over the pulpit by the audience of proud parents. First of all Russell loudly cleared his throat, showing everyone that his voice had changed. Then with a kick, he sent the bench flying out of the way. After that, he stepped up to the pulpit and presented his song. It actually went very well.

Soon after the end of school, we organized our trip to Mamarongo. Some of our family would go commercially, while the rest would fly directly to the airstrip at Cienega in the little Helio Courier where we would repack the little plane with lighter loads and the pilot would make shuttle flights from Cienega to our new strip in the Sierra. Our anticipation was high. What would we find upon our arrival?

"We urge you to consider showing the author your support by reviewing this book on both Amazon.com and Goodreads.com"